MEN AT THE CENTER:
REDEMPTIVE GOVERNANCE UNDER LOUIS IX

The Natalie Zemon Davis Annual Lecture Series
at Central European University, Budapest

MEN AT THE CENTER:
REDEMPTIVE GOVERNANCE
UNDER LOUIS IX

William Chester Jordan

Central European University Press

Budapest – New York

Published in 2012 by
Central European University Press
An imprint of the Central European University Limited Liability Company
Nádor utca 11, H-1051 Budapest, Hungary
Tel: +36-1-327-3138 or 327-3000 · *Fax:* +36-1-327-3183
E-mail: *ceupress@ceu.hu* · *Website*: *www.ceupress.com*

400 West 59th Street, New York NY 10019, USA
Tel: +1-212-547-6932 · *Fax:* +1-646-557-2416
E-mail: *mgreenwald@sorosny.org*

Cover design and layout by Péter Tóth

ISBN 978-615-5225-12-3
ISSN 1996-1197

Library of Congress Cataloging-in-Publication Data
Jordan, William C., 1948-
  Men at the center : redemptive governance under Louis IX / William
Chester Jordan.
     p. cm. — (The Natalie Zemon Davis annual lectures ; v. 11)
  Includes bibliographical references and index.
  ISBN 978-6155225123 (pbk.)
  1. France—Politics and government—1226-1270. 2. France—History—
Louis IX, 1226-1270. 3. Courts and courtiers—France—History—To 1500.
4. Courtesans—France—Biography. 5. Robert, of Sorbonne, 1201-1274. 6.
Boileau, Etienne, ca. 1200-1269. 7. Nesle, Simon de, ca. 1209-1279. I. Title.

  DC91.J76 2012
  944'.023—dc23

                        2012015686

Printed in Hungary by
Prime Rate Kft., Budapest

Table of Contents

Acknowledgements

I want to thank Gábor Klaniczay for inviting me to come to the Central European University (CEU) in Budapest in November 2011 to give the series of lectures on which this book is based. I have known Gábor almost as long as I have been a professor, and I have always admired and respected him. Thus, when he asked me to deliver the lectures, I was instantly predisposed to accept. My predisposition was strengthened even more by the opportunity I would have to honor my dear friend and former colleague Professor Natalie Zemon Davis, in whose honor the series is named. Natalie agreed to come to Budapest as well and to take part by commenting and raising questions generated from my presentations. While in Budapest we also met with graduate students of the CEU, learned of the interesting dissertation projects they had selected, and offered such advice as we could on how to pursue those projects. Many of these students attended the lectures

vii

and contributed by their questions and comments to the final form of the book. I wish to thank them and, indeed, all of those who offered stimulating responses to my arguments.

The experience was wholly positive, from the exquisite view of the castle across the Danube from the hotel, to the delicious meals, and to the welcome and hospitality in general. I know now that the organizing genius behind all of this was Csilla Dobos, the Academic and Ph.D. Program Coordinator for the Department of Medieval Studies at the CEU. There was never a question that I asked that she could not answer. There was never a request I made that she did not deal with effectively and efficiently. She went far beyond the call of duty by attending all the lectures! My gratitude to her knows no bounds.

I bounced many of my ideas off of several friends and colleagues at Princeton, including my wife Christine Kenyon Jordan, Professor John Haldon, two of my wonderful graduate students, Jenna Phillips and Hagar Barak, and the Academic Manager of the Department of History, Judith Hanson. None of them seemed to think the subject as I was developing it was entirely boring (hallelujah!), and this sustained me as I was crafting the talks. That said, one or more of them fairly often also challenged me to clarify points I was making and to keep to those points. They also endorsed my decision to name the series—and thus the book—"Men at the Center," a title meant to evoke Natalie's own scintillating work, *Women on the Margins: Three Seventeenth-Century Lives* (Cambridge, MA, and London: Harvard University Press, 1995), and the biographical approach she adopted in that work. When it turned out as I deepened my research that many of the men at the center whom I chose to discuss in the lectures had come from the margins of the French kingdom, socially and geographically, the symbolic evocation of Natalie's book came full circle. Of course, I dedicate the finished product, however insufficient, to her.

Chapter One

Robert of Sorbon, Churchman

Sorbon, today a tiny village of about two hundred souls, was very small in the thirteenth century. It is located in a region, the Ardennes, which has a rugged grandeur. The now defunct local journal, *Les Ardennes françaises*, devoted to the region's history, used as its motto, "Faisons connaître et admirer le Beau Pays d'Ardenne" ("Let us proclaim and gaze with pleasure on the beautiful Ardennes countryside"). Nevertheless, it was an economically unproductive land by the robust standards of most other regions in France in the thirteenth century. In part this was because the terrain of the Ardennes was rough and unwelcoming. Transport in and out of the hilly, boggy and heavily forested region was difficult. The too-compact soil produced hardwood trees that grew gnarled and were less desirable for lumber than those of many other regions, and such timber as woodsmen did harvest was, given the terrain, difficult to convey to major urban

1

markets or to ports for transshipment. Moreover, at the start of the thirteenth century the Ardennes was in many respects a lawless region, as traditional historians of the state conceive law, though not perhaps as a legal anthropologist would. For every society has rules and norms even in the absence of state authority. However, neither the royal government of France nor the administrations of any of the great seigneurs who claimed rights in the area could exercise them as they wanted to in peace.[1]

On either side of the year 1200 the Ardennes saw German, Flemish and French armies in conflict as part of two larger struggles then being waged. The first was between England and France and ultimately led to the English loss of Normandy and many of the other continental provinces to the king of France. The other was the warfare between supporters of Otto of Brunswick, on the one hand, and Philip of Swabia and, later, Frederick of Hohenstaufen and Pope Innocent III, on the other, over claims to the imperial throne. Germans and Flemings were either by direct monetary inducement or by political or economic commitment generally drawn more to the English side in the first conflict but they were woefully divided in the second. In any case, for all of these contending forces, the Ardennes and neighboring regions constituted a great and enduring arena in the opening two decades of the thirteenth century for bloodshed and death, for arson and pillage.

On October 9, 1201, a son was born in the village of Sorbon, in the heartland of the holdings of the count of Rethel, to a peasant couple who had him baptized Robert.[2] Almost nothing is known of the child's early life, except that he manifested a singular intelligence in the local schools, to the roisterous culture of which he seems to have made reference in comments later in life.[3] His parents, like so many other local parents, would have known the Ardennes of the period as a difficult place for advancement or, as we might say, for social mobility. And they would have known, like many others, that the best licit way for a peasant boy to improve his lot was to rise through the church. Robert of Sorbon[4] trained for the priesthood and rose steadily. He augmented his education, it has been suggested, by a period of instruction at the College of Ret(h)el in Paris, an association of scholars and economically disadvantaged students from the Rethélois, where he had passed his childhood years.[5]

His studies culminated in his becoming a secular master of theology, that is, a professor, at the University of Paris.[6] By about 1250 he had drawn and was drawing income, sequentially, from prebends he held as a canon of the cathedral of Notre-Dame of Cambrai and then as a canon of the cathedral of Notre-Dame of Paris.[7] Insofar as he was making a reputation in the capital, it was as a preacher and stern moralist denouncing gambling, the vernacular theater, bawdy songs, hypocrisy, prostitution, gossip, usury, lax attention to duty, pride in mastering theology, and generally being unchristian and thus doing the works of the Saracens.[8] He was, by training, versed in the works of Aristotle which were in vogue in the Paris schools, but in his own writings he drew more on the ancient philosopher's ethical than on his analytic and scientific works. Only in legendary retellings of his life, as Palémon Glorieux demonstrated, is Master Robert of Sorbon made to loom as large a philosophical and theological presence in thirteenth-century Paris as Bonaventure or Thomas Aquinas.[9] The modern afterlife of Robert in stories and monuments remains to be written.[10]

The unbending preacher with his message that popular amusements, like profane singing, was a diversion from faithful living and that the sacrament of confession should be at the center of the Christian moral experience came to the attention of King Louis IX (r. 1226–1270), himself the creator of a political regime that Jacques Le Goff has understandably called one of moral repression.[11] It did not impair Robert's chances of admission to and advancement in the royal court that the king's favorite devotional pastime was hearing sermons and even engaging in dialogue with preachers during their sermons.[12] This preacher's message—Robert's message—was particularly affecting. He condemned behavior, as noted, like frivolous composing and singing, which deviated from his narrow list of salutary pastimes, and he spoke of confession, a step on the way to forgiveness for such deviations, as a sacrament best practiced over a long period. One ought not to, he insisted, confess one's sins tersely to a priest, but at great length—in long therapy sessions, as it were—which provided opportunities for meditation, spiritual medication, and recuperation.[13] In a city in which the king lived almost next door to the cathedral and only a short walk from the schools, both of which were Robert's terrain of activity, it is unsurprising that the preacher should come to Louis's attention.

Scholarly efforts to see the king's brother Count Robert d'Artois as the preacher's sponsor may therefore be misguided.[14] True, the territorial heartland of Artois was little distant from the Ardennes, but it was not the Ardennes. His countship and the obligations of aristocratic largesse may have compelled the king's brother to act as the protégé of a few Artésiens but hardly of men from the Ardennais. Indeed, the theory that the count of Artois's influence was Robert of Sorbon's conduit to the royal court may owe something to later legends that the moralistic preacher was not actually a peasant after all, but the son of nobles

5

who had presumably fallen on hard times, a man whose innate nobility merely re-emerged into the bright light of day when changed circumstances permitted it to do so.[15] One is reminded of all the medieval stories, like *Robert the Devil* and *Havelock the Dane*, in which this is a prominent motif.[16] Humanists even speculated that the preacher was an otherwise unacknowledged brother of King Louis IX.[17] This would mean that the king's father Louis VIII had dallied with Robert of Sorbon's mother (wholly unattested and not even rumored in the thirteenth century). Or, the king's mother Blanche of Castile dallied with some fellow. All Robert of Sorbon ever said about his mother (he said it in a sermon) was that she was unlettered.[18] Of course, that Blanche of Castile was a well-educated woman, perhaps even the author of the words of a song in praise of the Blessed Virgin Mary, is no evidence against the humanists.[19] An illegitimate child could have been placed with an illiterate foster parent. Nevertheless, there is no evidence or contemporary or near-contemporary rumors of this.

By the year 1250 Robert of Sorbon did achieve admission to the royal court and indeed did so on his merits. He received the title *clerc du roi* and, probably somewhat later, *chapelain royal*. These designations described a quasi-official and regular attachment to the royal court, duties at religious services attended by the king, and frequent personal access to the monarch.[20] Despite Robert's obsession with confession, however, the allegation that he was Louis IX's regular confessor cannot be substantiated. Louis was one of the few laypeople (the Hungarian king was another) who had sought and received papal permission to select their own confessors from either the regular or secular clergy, including their chaplains, but the list of the French king's formally appointed confessors from 1248 on only includes Dominican friars.[21] Thus, the assertion that Robert of Sorbon served in this role may be another part of the legends that grew up after the chaplain's death. Nonetheless, it is generally agreed that whenever the king's usual confessors were absent or indisposed, he would turn to other clerical members of his retinue to assume this role. On occasion, then, Robert of Sorbon probably confessed the ruler, which may be the kernel of truth behind the legend.[22]

The signal adventures of Louis IX's life were his two crusades. He was absent from France in Cyprus, Egypt and the Holy Land from 1248 to 1254 and again in 1270, the year he died in the siege of Tunis. It was while the king was *outre-mer* in 1250 that Robert of Sorbon, who did not accompany him, first appears to have appealed for help in founding a college for poor boys who were students of theology. He would have made his appeal to Blanche of Castile, the queen-mother,

7

whom Louis had made regent for the period of his absence.[23] It is interesting that Blanche, too, shared the privilege with her son and his wife, Marguerite of Provence, of selecting her own confessor. Robert did not serve this role for either of the women, however. All the confessors that can be associated with the women of the royal house were Franciscan friars.[24] It may be churlish of me to suggest this, but I am of the opinion that Robert of Sorbon's reflections on confession were much admired at court. Yet, the actual practice of long and tedious, seemingly endless, periods of confession was not to everyone's liking or perhaps even possible for busy rulers.

The crown's money was largely committed in 1250 to the enormous expenditures for the crusade.[25] What Robert of Sorbon was seeking at this moment more than funding was the blessing of the royal court for his enterprise, a blessing, which might induce other men and women to contribute materially to his hopes and plans. In the long run, of course, he expected to get financial support not just good will from the crown, but as a courtier himself he could not have been insensible to the crush of obligations then facing the regency government. Money poured south to finance the crusade, to refill the king's coffers after his capture and the ransom of his army and for the repair of fortifications in the Holy Land. So difficult was the situation that Louis IX remarked that his treasury was nearly emptied temporarily by his obligations.[26]

Under the circumstances Robert of Sorbon's plans did not really get off the ground until three years after he first approached Blanche of Castile and then only in a very modest way. Palémon Glorieux traced with painstaking care the initial steps from 1253 to 1257, which truly mark the establishment of the Sorbonne, and its transformation into a real educational institution from what may have begun rather as a hospice.[27] The king's major contributions only began around the latter year and must be regarded as part of a general pattern of increased royal philanthropy.[28] For, his donations were occasioned by financial recovery from the expense of crusading, which I would estimate took at least two years from the time of the king's return to France in 1254. There is plenty of evidence of this time lag, such as Louis IX's repayment of a 5,000 pound *parisis* (l. p.) loan to the abbot of Cluny in 1256, two years after he contracted it, which was immediately after the completion of his sea voyage back from the Holy Land.[29] Endowments of money and property from Louis IX were good, but papal beneficence, even if limited to the realm of the spirit, was good too. And the two were connected. It must have been at least partly through the good offices of the king that so many popes— Alexander IV in 1259, Urban IV in 1261, and the king's personal friend Clement IV in 1268—were inclined to bless Robert's enterprise once Louis IX's philanthropy became known and to vest in the chaplain more or less absolute control as provisor over the new institution as long as he lived.[30]

Most of Robert of Sorbon's time in the late 1250s and the 1260s was occupied with fostering the growth of the college and ancillary projects related to it— redacting the statutes, establishing a preparatory program for students who were smart but came ill-prepared, and assiduously improving the library by purchase and by soliciting donors.[31] He did not abandon his other duties at the royal court and at Notre-Dame. His importance among the canons at the latter was recognized by his selection to represent the cathedral chapter after the death of Bishop Renaud Mignon de Corbeil, which is to say, he was one of the three canons who sought permission to elect a new bishop (the *licentia eligendi*).[32] Granting permission to elect was a privilege that pertained to the crown for replacement of abbots and bishops of regalian monasteries and sees.[33]

On September 29, 1270, two days before his sixty-ninth birthday, Robert redacted his last will and testament. A little more than one month before, on August 25, 1270, his supporter, Louis IX, had died on crusade. Upon his return from North Africa, the dead king's son, Philip III, began his rule. The nature of the court started to change, as the younger man came to depend on a favorite, Pierre de la Broce, who acquired an unsavory reputation. And even after Pierre's fall a few years later, the court did not resume its character as a center of austere holiness and the most extreme moral rigor. The young woman Philip III married (he had lost his first wife to disease on the crusade) and the young men, many of whom were her relatives, who occupied the new inner circle, were known for their attraction to the traditional and faddish chivalric pastimes.[34] The men in particular were fonder of hunting and warmongering than of austere piety. Some of the old king's advisers, like Mathieu of Vendôme, the abbot of Saint-Denis, survived the transition, even if their influence was muted for several years. But Robert of Sorbon passed away on August 15, 1274, before the favorite met his end and a small coterie of Louis IX's old advisers managed to regain some, if not all, the ground they had lost.[35]

Such, in brief, is the outline of Robert of Sorbon's life. He was a courtier in the formal sense of the word, but this implies more than mere service at the royal court. The existence of distinctly court cultures in medieval Europe has long been recognized. I have alluded already to the fundamental differences of mood and tone between the court of Louis IX and that of his son, Philip III. These differences manifested themselves not merely discursively or in terms of behavior and gesture. They also, through patronage, have been alleged to affect the arts, as Robert Branner's work on the court style under Louis IX long ago argued. But until recently historians have not even had a good sense of the extent and composition of Louis IX's court. We have known about some key people, if they were famous in other ways, but no one, again until recently, has tried to map the boundaries, personnel and duties of courtiers with the kind of precision that would satisfy. With the research of the archivist Jean-François Moufflet on the *hôtel du roi* in the reign of Louis IX, we are heading in the right direction, but he has been the first to admit that we are still far from the goal.[36]

Robert of Sorbon is famous enough as the founder of his college to command the attention of scholars interested in the history of the University of Paris. He is famous enough as a preacher, moralist and defender of sacramental confession to command the attention of students of sermons, cultural representations and devotional practices. Nevertheless, little has been made of his actual work at court. Rather historians have contented themselves with repeating the few candid anecdotes about him that have come down to us from the most famous source, Jean de Joinville's *Life of Saint Louis*. Though not properly regarded as a courtier himself, Jean de Joinville, the *sénéchal* of Champagne, knew the king from the early 1240s, and he accompanied Louis IX on his first crusade from 1248 to 1254, though not on his second in 1270, which he opposed because of the king's weak health.[37] The *sénéchal* was an intermittent visitor to court, however, after Louis's first crusade and was routinely admitted to the royal circle of friends whenever he was there.[38] His memoir reveals his sometimes fractious relationship with Robert of Sorbon.

The preacher and the aristocrat ordinarily enjoyed each other's conversation. Once when they were speaking *sotto voce* at the royal table, where, Jean de Joinville mentions, Robert often took his meals at Louis IX's request, the king cautioned them to speak more loudly so that they would not incur the suspicions of others. On a second occasion, the *sénéchal* also mentions that the king "in a playful mood" (*en joie*) provoked a debate between Robert and himself (Jean) over whether a *prud'homme* or a *béguin* was the better sort of man. Robert had a reputation as a *prud'homme*, a virtuous sort of man of action, according to Jean, but the chaplain did not see that this made living the life of a *béguin*, that is, of a contemplative man (Jacques Monfrin translates the word into modern French as *dévot*) less preferred. Again, Louis IX intruded himself into the conversation to praise and offer his preference for the life of a *prud'homme*, thereby and at one level flattering Robert of Sorbon's *prud'homie*. This flattery, it should be pointed out, was in no way compromised by the fact that the king also frankly admired and generously supported the mendicant friars and therefore implicitly various forms of the devoted life.[39]

On a third occasion, the royal chaplain criticized the *sénéchal* for upstaging the king by wearing fancier clothing than Louis. Jean retorted with a defense of his privilege to wear the aristocratic dress bestowed on him by his parents and implicitly appropriate to his lineage, irrespective of what the king wore. He in turn admonished Robert for dressing above his station and in finer cloth than the king wore at the time because the preacher was the offspring of peasants (*de vilain et de vilainne*). The argument got out of hand, necessitating the king's intervention and his defense of the royal chaplain in order to counteract the humiliating reference to his base origins. But, then, out of the chaplain's hearing Louis confessed to the *sénéchal* and the royal son and son-in-law, who had overheard, that he actually thought Master Robert had been wrong to criticize Jean.[40]

These are wonderful anecdotes, but scholars, even the best of them, have usually just cited or quoted rather than analyzed them perceptively.[41] What can one learn? As to the arguments that Robert may have presented about *prud'homie* and devotion, Nicole Bériou has given a brilliant if speculative reconstruction from the evidence of his sermons.[42] I am more interested in what the anecdotes suggest about Robert of Sorbon's personality. The master, the *clerc du roi*, the royal chaplain, the great preacher, the stern moralist was a courtier, but he was also ashamed of his origins, if one takes the anecdotes seriously. He liked to be flattered, and the king recognized it—and flattered him. The king seemed to know instinctively that a man of Robert's origins, no matter his repute as a scholar, preacher or defender of highly disciplined behavior, needed regular confirmation of the status he had achieved as a courtier.[43] What this suggests, in turn, is that part of Louis IX's kingship, a part I do not believe has ever been fully appreciated, is the way he balanced personalities at court. It must have been a considerable effort when visitors, like Jean de Joinville, who could not have fully appreciated how strenuous this continuous effort was, blustered their way, even good-naturedly, into the activities of the court circle—speaking, as if in secrets, with courtiers which might inspire concern and apprehension in others. This is the force, I take it, of Louis IX's caution to Robert and Jean not to speak *sotto voce* at the crowded royal dinner table, and it is the reason the *sénéchal* later, realizing his mistake and the king's craft, chose to retell it.

15

We also see by means of these anecdotes that Louis IX wanted Robert as a courtier. Hearing of his prowess as a preacher and of his moral temperament was what got the *maître* access to the king in the first instance, and it mirrors by the way how Louis, when he returned from crusade, became interested in the Franciscan friar Hugues of Digne, although Hugues stubbornly refused to join the royal court.[44] But what explains the chaplain's staying power? There must have been more, especially since we know he was not particularly sought after in practice as a father confessor.

So, what was it or, perhaps in the plural, what were the traits or the abilities that assured Robert a continuing place at the royal court, implying the favor of Louis IX, and by doing so allowed him to exploit networks of power and patronage that gave his pet project, the Sorbonne, such an advantageous commencement and early history? No doubt there were many, but there are three that I think deserve special emphasis— the first, which I have already hinted at, may be called moral, the second philanthropic and the third governmental. Before discussing them, however, it would be wise to make the case that Master Robert actually did successfully exploit the court circle in establishing and sustaining the Sorbonne.

The evidence is very strong. The names of most of the early endowers of and donors to the Sorbonne are those of men from within, indeed, sometimes from within the most intimate ranks of, the court circle.[45] Such a one was Guillaume of Chartres, who endowed the Sorbonne through the conveyance of a number of Parisian properties, but who seems to have had lower class non-noble origins. At one time in his life, after joining the church, Guillaume drew income from a canonry in Saint-Quentin. In some way (perhaps through the good offices of the queen's physician, whom I will be discussing momentarily), he came to the king's attention and was asked to serve at court, like Robert of Sorbon, as a royal chaplain. He ultimately became a Dominican friar, but though the Dominicans were formally the Order of Friars Preachers, modern critics have not thought much of Guillaume's surviving sermons: "Ils ne méritent aucunement d'être publiés," one has written about them.[46] It is not known what Louis IX thought of the sermons, but there is no doubt what he thought of the man. Guillaume of Chartres went on serious missions for Louis IX, accompanied him on both of the king's crusades and served him as chaplain and, later, confessor. Indeed, he was with the king when he was captured on his first crusade and when he died on his second. A short chronicle Guillaume wrote adds to our already abundant evidence on Louis's rule. Like Robert he exploited his contacts in the royal circle, endeavoring around 1277 to get his nephew received into the royal monastery of Saint-Denis, whose abbot was Mathieu of Vendôme who had been one of Louis IX's closest legal and political advisers. Mathieu served as co-regent when the king went on his final crusade. Guillaume of Chartres died in 1280.[47]

The second of this group was the physician, Robert of Douai, another man of obscure origins, who early on in his ecclesiastical career (he was in orders by 1245) became a canon of Senlis and Saint-Quentin as well. It is their mutual Saint-Quentin connection that makes me think that Robert of Douai may have been Guillaume of Chartres's conduit to court. However that may be, Robert of Douai made a considerable reputation as a *medicus* and managed to obtain an appointment as a royal physician and, indeed, ultimately as Queen Marguerite's personal physician, a fact he proudly noted in his will dated 1258. In 1254 he had sold a house to Guillaume of Chartres, one of the properties that the latter subsequently conveyed to the Sorbonne.[48] Around the same time he was called upon by Pope Innocent IV to help negotiate some of the strife then affecting relations between the mendicant and secular masters at the University of Paris.[49] Clearly, he had sufficient fame and significant interest in educational institutions, or in this educational institution, to have been approached for this task. The bequests in

Robert's will provided a windfall for the new College of the Sorbonne when he died on the 25th of May 1258. It received 1,500 l. p., a genuinely princely sum, as well as Robert's theology books for its nascent library.

The enormous size of this bequest helps explain Robert of Douai's unsavory reputation in some quarters, quarters outside the royal circle. Poems and songs constituted a major medium in the High Middle Ages for slurring one's enemies or people whose behavior was allegedly repugnant. Robert of Douai appears in Henri d'Andeli's contemporary poem known as the "Battle of the Seven Arts." In it he is upbraided as a money-hungry practitioner, equivalent to a surgeon.[50] Again, one must ask what there was about the doctor that attracted a king who was so sensitive to avarice. Did Louis IX know of Robert of Douai's reputation outside the royal circle? And, if he did, did he care? Would he have simply assumed that a man who served as the queen's physician was entitled to the considerable financial benefits of the office, even if he was a little too proud and thus encouraged screeds meant to denigrate him? That Robert of Douai's obit was celebrated at the Sorbonne, the abbey of Sainte-Geneviève, and the convent of the Mathurins (Trinitarians) of Paris does suggest, however, that no matter how greedy he appeared to certain possibly envious detractors, he was lavish in his largesse to educational and religious institutions.[51]

Two other key persons in supporting Robert of Sorbon's enterprise in its earliest phase of existence and in sustaining succeeding popes' blessings of the institution (they became cardinals) were Geoffroy of Bar and Guillaume of Bray. Their origins mirror Robert of Sorbon's own and the origins of Guillaume of Chartres and Robert of Douai. Geoffroy of Bar, though he rose to be dean of the cathedral chapter of Paris, a courtier in Louis IX's entourage and cardinal-priest of Santa-Susanna, was born into a commoner family living in abject poverty.[52] And Guillaume of Bray was from another family of 'nobodies'; yet, he, too, found his way to a deanship at the cathedral of Notre-Dame of Laon—in the Ardennes—where he also served as *officialis*, typically a legal expert, and to Louis IX's court, ending his career as cardinal-priest of San-Marco.[53] All of these men would have served as examples for the impoverished students who came to the Sorbonne, examples of what hard work, determination, a great deal of learning, and supercharged piety could bring them under suitable circumstances and under a suitable master like Louis IX.

Louis IX's suitability extended to his ambivalent attitude toward social class. He was sensitive to the feelings of those who were high-born, as one can infer from one of the anecdotes Jean de Joinville related and that I have retold. The king both consoled the low-born Robert of Sorbon when Jean made reference to the chaplain's humble rustic origins and reassured his own high-born son, son-in-law and the *sénéchal* that they were right to display their elevated status. There is nonetheless a weirdness even in this otherwise seemingly straightforward anecdote, for in making his point separately to his aristocratic audience, the king added—quite unnecessarily—that they should array themselves nicely and appropriately so as to intensify their wives' love of them and their dependents' esteem for them. This assertion or even exhortation came from a king who had a running battle with critics of his plain style of dress ("Friar Louis" they mocked him outside of his hearing) and especially with his queen, Marguerite, a woman who complained that he dressed inappropriately and below his station. This encouragement to his noble listeners to dress well was expressed, one should remember, by a king who responded to his wife's criticism by taunting her with the bitter irony of promising that he would dress as she wished him to if she would agree to dress as he desired her to, a remark which presumably made her angry but also demonstrated the utter futility of pursuing further dialogue on the matter with her husband.[54]

My own view is that the king relished the feelings of generosity generated by bestowing blessings on the low-born clerics. It is true, perhaps, that his behavior ran the risk of coming across to others as condescending and rather off-putting. Yet, there are also a sufficient number of indications that his own personal endurance of humiliation, self-imposed, such as flagellation or plainness of dress, or imposed by circumstances, such as his failure on his first crusade, helped soften the impression.[55] "Dear children," he once told an audience of Dominican novices in Paris slightly before he swore the formal vow to undertake another crusade, "praise our Lord and do not pine for the joys of the world. I have been king for forty years and have had more joys than all of you together, that I know. And in all my days, I did not spend one full day, that was not mingled with sorrow."[56]

I noted that the kind of influence that Robert of Sorbon enjoyed emanated largely from his obvious closeness—the public knowledge of his closeness—to the king. This closeness had many aspects, and I noted above that three of them may not be fully appreciated to the degree or depth they should be. I believe they exemplify the two men's common moral, philanthropic, and governmental sensibilities. As to the moral sensibility, it is instantiated in their mutual distaste for profane songs. Ironically this grew out of their love of songs, but those of Christian worship. Let us remind ourselves of the extraordinary emphasis laid in Christian worship on singing as a proper expression of love for God. This was rooted in scripture itself. "Sing unto the lord a new song" (Psalms 96:1 [Vulgate 95:1], and elsewhere)—indeed all the Psalms, not to mention the Song of Songs, testify to this sentiment. Profane songs struck the two men as inappropriate, and on occasion, in their bawdy form, genuinely obscene, akin to blasphemy, a topic that will be addressed in Chapter Three.

Earlier it was noted that there is a thirteenth-century vernacular song whose lyrics are attributed *in the thirteenth century* to Louis IX's mother Blanche of Castile. I adduced this as evidence of her education or, rather, of the reputation she had for literacy of a high order. Neither musicologists nor historians have been entirely persuaded by the attribution, despite its earliness, and I do not want to pursue the subject here. But it is germane to repeat that this vernacular song was a Marial hymn, words written to praise the Blessed Virgin. This is germane because there is another song. And it was attributed to Louis IX himself, although historians and musicologists have been equally lukewarm about accepting this also early attribution.[57] I do not insist that Louis IX had anything to do with this song except that it came to be "associated" with him, as one scholar put it—put it quite weakly.[58] The lyrics are more complex than those of the wholly French song attributed to the king's mother. French and Latin lines alternate in a long sixteen-verse poem.[59] The alternating French lines make a clipped sort of poem themselves. The alternating Latin lyrics do so as well. The French and Latin together make a profoundly expressive poem. The Latin is comprised of formulaic phrases extracted from formal devotional poetry, hymns and the liturgy. The French draws on formulas and conventions of vernacular *trouvère* love poetry. Whoever put these lyrics together displayed great sophistication; it is quite an impressive accomplishment.[60]

Two facts: it, too, is a Marial song, like the one attributed to Blanche of Castile, and it was, again to use the weakest formulation, associated with Louis IX around his own time.[61] Indeed, it was said to have been the song the king, who sang devotional songs, attempted to persuade those around him, who enjoyed and indulged profane songs, to sing in their stead.[62] Although I cannot prove it, I believe there is reasonably strong evidence that to this association with Louis IX one can add Robert of Sorbon's partial or co-authorship of the extremely sophisticated and allusive lyrics.

One morning in the month of May, the poets or poet writes, the protagonist set out for a meadow intending to chant the psalms (*psal*mos *intendens psallere*), and he encountered the Virgin Mother.

L'autrier matin el moys de may
regis *et*erni munere
que par un matin me levay
mundum proponens fugere.
*e*n un plesant pre m'en entray
psal*m*os intendens psallere:
la mere *d*ieu ilec trouvay
jam lucis orto sidere.

This first stanza, I hope, gives some flavor of the poetry. The words reveal more than may at first be apparent. To give one example: the last line of this stanza, *jam lucis orto sidere,* "now the star of light [the sun] having risen," is the incipit of one of the most famous hymns in the Latin church, the hymn which was sung in the early morning of the first day of the week. It had not been chosen by our thirteenth-century poet or poets merely because the scansion and the rhyme work with the other Latin lines. They do work, but this ancient hymn has its own point that mirrors and thus makes even more emphatic the sentiments of our thirteenth-century poem, whose protagonist was intending to sing psalms (*psalmos intendens psallere*) in the early morning, at daybreak, at the very sunrise (*jam lucis orto sidere*). Moreover, in the fifth line of the ancient hymn's first verse, the author of the original implores God, *Nil lingua . . . peccet,* "Let not [my] tongue sin." In other words, he asks God to prevent him from using his gift of voice, which I would gloss as singing, in vain.

In the following three stanzas of the thirteenth-century song, the poet extols the Virgin's beauty, compares her to a rose, her clothing to the soft coverings of budding flowers and her perfect teeth favorably to crystal (*comme la rose entre la gent / in gemmis grato tegmine. / plus que cristal sont blanc li dent*).[63] In stanza five and six her angelic character is highlighted as well as the glow of peace that emanates from her visage. *Douce Dame*, the classic chivalric mode of salutation, is how she is addressed, this virginal flower, who inspires good works. And then by stanza eight the tone changes to that of a sinner begging for help, for counsel and for salvation through the intervention of the *gloriosa domina*. This appeal allows her to invoke her Son as well as the Holy Spirit (*veni creator spiritus*) as those hypostases of the godhead that will redeem the sinner. The Virgin is *Mater misericordie*, the mother of mercy, in effecting this divine intervention, which in turn lifts the poet to a state of heavenly bliss. And then the images of redemption cascade in line after line, stanza after stanza: a floral shower, beautiful songs, the nightingale, heavenly choruses, the salvific sign of the cross and, finally, the Virgin's commendation of the poet, her devoted slave (*mon devot serf*), to her Son. As the encounter ends with the Virgin ascending into heaven, the poet—but who is the poet? Let us assume for a moment that the poet speaks the words or the merged words of Louis IX (was not King David the reputed author of the psalms?) and Robert of Sorbon. The poet requests the Virgin always to keep him in her sight, to protect him from the devil's seductions, and to bring him when he passes beyond human life to celestial paradise.

> Mere de dieu, vrai salut port
> fons pietate maxime,
> de celui m'envois confort
> salutem prestans anime.
> garde moi de l'anemi fort
> qui me temptat sepissime;
> paradis m'otroit a la mort
> rerum creator optime.
>   amen.

The final line of the thirteenth-century lyrics, *rerum creator optime*, is the best evidence of Robert of Sorbon's hand at work in the song. The line is the incipit of the early medieval hymn that was used throughout the Middle Ages and beyond for Wednesday matins in the divine office. As one might expect, the old hymn mimics the sentiments of the last stanza of the thirteenth-century poem. The protagonist desires God's help to be vigilant in the struggle against sin. But the specific mode of behavior which the hymnist pledges in order to induce the Lord to bestow divine protection is in itself revealing in that it elegantly and precisely coheres with the moral and sacramental vision of Robert of Sorbon: *Te, sancte Christe, poscimus; / ignosce tu criminibus, / ad confitendum surgimus / morasque noctis rumpimus* (Holy Christ, we beg thee, / forgive our sins, / we arise [in the morning] to confess them / and we break through the interval of night). Which is to say, we confess and confess and confess— at length, all day and into the night—just as the founder of the Sorbonne had preached and written his whole life as a priest. The song that commenced in the early morning in the month of May thus ends with an allusion to the night, which threatens, but can be overcome, by persistent, continuous confession.

In the same way devotional singing, I infer, was understood to be capable of overcoming the evils generated by profane singing. That this interpretation may be correct I offer as parallel evidence the famous Psalter of Saint Louis, produced for Louis IX around 1260.[64] In the Psalter there is a sequence of seventy-eight Old Testament illustrations. These magnificent illustrations have excited much interest over the years.

It is not so much the iconography of one of the illustrations that is relevant as its allusion to the fuller text it evokes. The First Book of the Kings, chapters one and two (I Samuel 1–2), tells the story, illustrated schematically in the Psalter (fol. 67 v.), of Hannah the barren wife of Elkanah. She prayed God to give her a son and vowed him to the Lord's service, if her prayer was granted. The prophet Eli saw her praying silently but fervently moving her lips and decided she had to be intoxicated (I Samuel 1:12). But she explained herself. When she was subsequently rewarded with a son, Samuel, the future prophet, she prayed a prayer of gratitude, which is known as the Song of Hannah (I Samuel 2:2–10). The trope, the power of devotional words (singing) over other words, is the same as can be inferred from the last stanza of the thirteenth-century song, *L'autrier matin el moys de may*. As Hannah puts it, "my mouth is enlarged over my enemies . . . . Do not multiply to speak lofty things, boasting; let old matters depart from your mouth" (I Samuel 2:1, 3). The sentiment, then, was expressed in another manuscript, which generations of scholars have argued reflect the very essence of Louis IX's religious views.

If *L'autrier matin el moys de may* is a song which served to challenge the practice of profane singing in Louis IX's court and also so well captures the similar guiding moral principles and impulses of the king and Robert of Sorbon, there is another sensibility that I called philanthropic that bound them as well. It concerns the *béguines*. The whole subject of the *béguines* as it pertains to the French court and which is vital to an understanding of how a man like Robert, born on the margins, could effectively establish himself at the center of the realm, has been put on a new footing by the work of Professor Tanya Stabler Miller. In a data rich and richly evocative dissertation on the *béguinage* of Paris directed by Professor Sharon Farmer of the University of California at Santa Barbara and drawing creatively on northern French and Flemish sermon collections, Stabler Miller has overturned a plethora of received opinions.[65] I have no wish to steal her thunder from her as yet unpublished book, but I do need to borrow two points from her already published articles in order to make my case about Robert of Sorbon, the first point dealing with the origin of the Paris *béguinage* and the second with the spiritual welfare of its inmates.[66]

As to the origin of the Paris *béguinage*, the institution was not generated from below. There were laywomen called *béguines* who dressed plainly and lived holy though non-professed lives in tiny communities of two, three or four individuals in thirteenth-century Paris.[67] They had not presented a petition to Louis IX asking for the establishment of a building complex that would house hundreds of such women together, to be organized under a head mistress.[68] Indeed, many of these women in their tiny communities scattered over the city continued to live quite successfully apart from the great *béguinage*, which the king founded in 1264.[69] This institution literally required urban redevelopment on a colossal scale and aggressive recruitment of women, perhaps as many as four hundred, to the establishment.[70] Louis IX got the idea after he visited Ghent and saw a large, well-organized *béguinage* or so later traditions allege, or perhaps he simply heard an enthusiastic report on it.[71] What makes the inspiration of the Ghent example plausible is the presence of so many men in the king's entourage who came from the Franco-Flemish borderlands, including Robert of Sorbon himself, Robert of Douai, and Guillaume of Bray, whose service in the Ardennais see of Laon has already been noticed. Whether or not Louis saw the Ghent *béguinage* or had been specifically informed of it, he would have heard about similar institutions scattered about the region, though perhaps not as large as Ghent's. One of these, one on which Louis IX bestowed alms, was Cambrai's. It is worth recalling that Robert of Sorbon had held a canonry at the cathedral of Cambrai and, as Nicole Bériou points out, knew the *béguinage* there.[72]

31

When the king decided to introduce such an institution to Paris, he stinted not in the least in the effort or the material resources to do so. And there is not the slightest doubt that the enterprise was strongly supported by Robert of Sorbon and helped seal the alliance between him and the king. All of a sudden, thanks to Stabler Miller's work, one prominent theme in Master Robert's sermons, a theme which praised the laudatory nature of these women's style of living, makes more sense.[73] Moreover, the bond between king and chaplain received a fillip in that Robert's defense of *béguines* flew in the teeth of the Parisian professor, Guillaume of Saint-Amour's recent criticisms of mendicant and *béguine* styles of living in the 1250s.[74] So harsh was his criticism, so annoying, with its apocalyptical overtones, and, finally, so obviously directed against Louis IX's own sensibilities that the king worked hard and successfully to secure a papal condemnation of Guillaume's works and his perpetual exile from Paris.[75]

Yet, this is not the end of the story. Stabler Miller, led by the example of other scholars, like Nicole Bériou, has undertaken the painstaking examination of sermons by Sorbonnistes, including Robert, and sermons directed to or commenting on *béguine* life in the first century of the Sorbonne's existence.[76] She and they have demonstrated that it fell significantly to the Sorbonnistes along with the Dominicans to provide, partly through their sermons, for the spiritual welfare of the women in the *Grand Béguinage* of Paris.[77] *Béguines* came under heightened scrutiny and received more public and official criticism, including papal, after Louis IX's death.[78] But it is indicative of the intimate association of the crown with and, in particular, the legacy of Saint Louis at both the Sorbonne and the *Grand Béguinage* that the latter institution escaped the censures that so many other *béguinages*, large and small, endured in the fourteenth century.[79] I cannot commend Tanya Stabler Miller's work enough.

Besides the similar moral views on music and the similar philanthropic impulse toward the *béguines* shared by Louis IX and Robert of Sorbon, a third bond, as noted before, arose from what might be called a perceived similarity in the two men's notions of governance. Men liked to claim to have influenced Louis IX in the governmental and administrative practices he instituted or they liked merely to praise the practices themselves and his choices of the men to enforce them. Jean de Joinville asserted that it was he (Jean) who cautioned the king once about receiving a gift from the abbot of Cluny who had a matter before the royal court. The *sénéchal* went so far as to suggest that the king listened to the abbot's case more favorably as a result, and, Jean says, the king thought it over and had to agree that the *sénéchal* was right. It was this revelation that induced Louis IX, again according to Jean, to issue rules limiting the gifts that councilors could accept, one provision of the great ordinances of reform that the king instituted in 1254 upon returning from his first crusade.[80] Elsewhere Jean and others simply gloried in the king's appointments of moral rigorists to important offices, even if their social profile diverged from what one might have expected of a king of the Franks, for, strange to tell, he might appoint foreigners.[81] Yet, though much might be and has been surmised we know very little apart from Jean de Joinville's possibly extravagant praise of himself as to who specifically counseled Louis in these matters. Astute the king may have been, ever alert to hear about people who might be useful, but who took part in the inner administrative councils?

No serious scholar, so far as I know, has really pressed the notion that Robert of Sorbon, despite being a courtier, was in these inner *administrative* councils. Perhaps the royal chaplain's general views mimicked the king's, but what evidence is there that his influence went further or that anyone thought it did? One way to rephrase this question is to ask, whom did Louis's subjects praise or blame for the policies he articulated and enforced? A neglected source for answering this question is a criticism of royal policies found in a contemporary song. The song is a screed aimed at Louis IX's legislation, legislation perceived by some aristocrats as undermining their power and prestige.[82]

This satirical song appears to have had as its author a disgruntled baron or the lyricist personates the voice of one who thought the apparatus of investigation into the administration of baronial justice which the king had set up essentially deprived him of his traditional authority: he would have preferred to remain, in the words of the song, "le maître de [son] fief."[83] And whom did he blame for this state of affairs, this assault on Sweet France, *Douce France* (his phrase)?[84] In truth, he did not blame the king. God forbid! The king, he believed, would have come to his senses but for the baleful influence of his clerical councilors.[85] The poet laments that even Robert of Sorbon, if the identification made by Leroux de Lincy, the editor of the song, is correct, did not caution the king. Robert was too beholden to other clerics, in the poet's words, those (*li vostre*, or *partisans* in the editor's modern French translation) whose support he was cultivating presumably for his college—he was too beholden to them to admonish and restrain Louis IX.[86] And so, the barons in the poet's moral universe were reduced to confronting, resenting and resisting an unnatural alliance of charity (*aumosne*)—alms for poor boys at the Sorbonne and for holy women at the *béguinage* will serve—an unnatural alliance of charity, on the one

35

hand, and sin (*péchié*), on the other, sin implicitly being the assault on their noble privileges.[87]

If Robert was the object of the poet's critique, as Leroux de Lincy argued, would he have been moved by it? Unlikely. He deliberately chose to adhere to the king's and his own friends' views. In part, one supposes, this was instrumental. He wished to stay in favor at court and cultivate other courtiers in support of the Sorbonne. But everything that can be inferred from the sources also suggests a man zealous for discipline—the discipline of personal behavior and the construction and maintenance of a disciplined society. Disciplined governance and the expectation of disciplined governance from others possessing judicial and administrative authority—all in the service of the redemption of the realm—were subsets of this mentality, a mentality Robert of Sorbon shared fully with his lord and master, King Louis IX of France.

In Chapters Two and Three, I hope to show that in Étienne Boileau and Simon de Nesle the king found equally fervent, some might even say fanatical devotees who willingly walked in his ways.

Chapter Two

Étienne Boileau, Bourgeois

Like most of the men whom we met in Chapter One, the central figure of this chapter has obscure origins. "On ignore toutesfois la naissance et l'origine de cet Estienne Boileau," as Dom Michel Félibien declared in the early eighteenth century in his monumental *Histoire de la ville de Paris*.[1] Because, however, Étienne Boileau became such an iconic figure in the history of the royal administration as *prévôt* of Paris, several families of aristocratic stock that possessed similar surnames invented genealogies in the centuries to come that made him a great and noble progenitor.[2] Such was the case of the family of Marie-Louis-Joseph de Boileau, a mayor of Abbeville in 1782, who came originally from Dunkirk and was an *écuyer* (squire) and lord of the infinitesimally small seigneurie of Tenède.[3] Many similar claims were based on forged documents which were exposed by a series of gifted late nineteenth- and early twentieth-century scholars, most notably

Léopold Delisle, the erudite conservateur-en-chef of the manuscript collection of the Bibliothèque nationale.[4] Unfortunately the sketch of Étienne Boileau's life in the usually dependable and often authoritative *Histoire littéraire de la France* was published before some of these early modern forgeries were fully exposed, and so it has taken a long time for the truth to prevail.[5]

What is the truth, if one may take such a positivist approach to the evidence? There seems little reason to doubt that Étienne was of modest birth. The first known mentions of him apart from his holding the office of *prévôt* of Paris are as *prévôt* of Orléans in 1259 and 1260.[6] What was a *prévôt*? The word applied to offices in the clerical hierarchy and lay administration. It is the latter that is relevant here.[7] The office changed over time, but in the eleventh and twelfth centuries *prévôts* were at base estate managers. The word could be used for such men whether they worked for kings, for aristocrats or for institutions. By the thirteenth century royal *prévôts* had moved beyond merely managing the king's property in the narrow sense. Under the *baillis*, the fifteen to twenty or so great regional administrators who commanded huge salaries and ran the country in the king's name, the *prévôts* had emerged as administrators of concentrated blocks of royal rights and properties, and they were headquartered in major towns. They reported to the *baillis* for the audit of their accounts and for review of their administration in general.[8] Lesser rights of justice and the police powers implied by such rights were entrusted to *prévôts*, while high or capital justice—the right to punish by dismemberment or death—tended to be restricted to the *baillis*.[9]

This is not to say that all capital justice lay with the crown's *baillis*. Much of it had devolved over the Middle Ages to individual seigneurs as well as to corporate lords, like cathedral chapters, abbeys, and towns. Nonetheless, what still lay with the crown was very considerable and was administered by its own judicial officials. In the thirteenth century these included the king himself through his judges in the *Parlement* or High Court of Paris. It also included an array of other High Courts, variously called *Parlements*, *Jours* or *Echiquiers*—courts of great territorial baronies that had lost their independence to or been regained by the crown (the word French scholars have used is *rattachement*). Although the *baillis* administered royal, including capital, justice in the provinces, both their criminal and their civil judgments were subject to review by the appropriate High Courts and occasionally were reviewed.[10]

At the beginning of the thirteenth century, the *prévôts*, with the exception of a few hereditary office holders, were commoners and revenue farmers;

they had bid for and won their positions by making the highest competitive bids.[11] Whatever the profits of justice which they collected during their administration and which exceeded what they had bid for their office was a substantial part of their 'remuneration.' So, *prévôts* had a very strong incentive to be aggressive and unbending in the enforcement of royal rights. They also had an incentive to overstep their legitimate powers whenever they thought their remuneration was inadequate.[12] Louis IX in the course of his reign instituted a whole set of investigative mechanisms intended to protect his subjects against unwarranted exploitation by *prévôts* and their subordinates (sub-*prévôts*, sergeants, and sub-sergeants), most of whose positions were farmed.[13] The king also experimented with paying salaries to these *prévôts* and their subordinates, but the experiment was limited by the drawdown of other obligations on royal revenues.[14]

Étienne Boileau was the royal *prévôt* of Orléans in 1259 and 1260. He was presumably a revenue farmer while exercising this office. If his status was typical, he was a commoner. He may have been a native of Orléans and connected to the important burgher family with the Boileau eponym that held offices in municipal administration there.[15] Although months after his death he was explicitly referred to as a knight, this was, as we shall see, probably a courtesy.[16] Certainly nobody in Étienne's lifetime made reference to his 'good birth.' All that we know of his career shows him working in towns, interacting with bourgeois, and administering urban affairs. In what town, if any, he formally possessed citizenship, however, is unknown.

Étienne, as noted, was *prévôt* of Orléans in 1259 and 1260. Beyond this simple statement, nothing is known of the specific accomplishments he made in the office or in other offices he may have held before then. What is known is that his reputation as a capable and honest administrator was very high when he was chosen late that year or early the next for the office of *prévôt* of Paris.[17] This was the one *prévôté* that broke the mold. Paris was both the largest town in the kingdom by several orders of magnitude, and it was for all intents and purposes also the capital city.[18] In terms of importance and the challenges to be faced this put the *prévôt* of Paris in a class by himself.

Jean de Joinville in a famous passage of the *Vie de saint Louis* described Paris as a seething cauldron of crime and injustice before Étienne's appointment as *prévôt* and a paradise after he disciplined the town by the scrupulous exercise specifically of capital justice— the infliction of the death penalty—an option, one knows, not widely available to other *prévôts*. I will return to this passage and quote it at length in a moment. Before doing so, however, it is worth looking at another of Jean's stories, which refers to an incident that occurred in Paris after the king swore the crusader's vow but before departing on crusade, so between late 1244 and mid-1248. The *sénéchal* was on his way to Paris at the time and remembered seeing three dead men being carried to the king in a cart. They had been killed by a cleric in minor orders whom they had robbed. Louis IX, when he later met the cleric, told him that his shedding of blood debarred him from achieving ordination as a priest but was impressive in its own way, for the cleric's deed really showcased his prowess as an archer and a swordsman. Indeed, the king told him that he would employ him as a crusader; Louis IX needed such men.[19]

The dark humor here belies the fuller and much grislier narrative line of the story. The three dead men were royal sergeants, policemen, as it were, who worked under the aegis of the *prévôt* of Paris. They were in the habit of hanging out in Paris's backstreets, in wait for likely targets from whom they could steal money and goods. They encountered one, the cleric, on a moonlit night and humiliated him by stripping him of his clothes, all of his clothes except his undergarment. The cleric went home and armed himself with a crossbow, while a boy got his sword for him. Then the cleric hunted down the thieves and killed them—an arrow in the heart of one, slicing through the leg of another who then bled to death, and, after catching up with the last one in a stranger's house where he had tried to find refuge, he split his skull with a sword blow down to the teeth. The cleric told onlookers what he had done and why and then turned himself in.

How do we know that the house to which the last robber fled was not the house of a friend but that of a stranger? We know because the story I have just related and which Jean de Joinville heard and retold in the *Vie de saint Louis* was in fact the information culled from a short investigation by the then-*prévôt* of Paris. It was he who had to admit that men in his own employ had been the malefactors. It was he who had to show the king the evidence, the mangled sanguinary bodies, for the cart with the corpses had been brought to rest in front of the royal palace. The king saw the cart, the *prévôt*, the cleric, and the crowd of bystanders the next morning when, of all things, he was emerging from the royal chapel (given the date, this was the new and astonishingly beautiful Sainte-Chapelle). This is the context for the *prévôt*'s presentation, which was a kind of abasing self-indictment of the insufficiency of his control of his own men. It is the context for the king's remarkable leniency, for ultimately the guilty sergeants were his men, too. And, finally, it is the context for the shouts of approval and God speed to the royal crusader that went up from the bystanders when Louis explained his leniency. "I would have you know," he said, "that this is because I strongly desire my people to see that I will not uphold them in any of their wrong-doings."[20] The people he was referring to were his officials. In modern words, Louis IX was actually saying, I shall not take retribution against anyone for killing my men if they wrongfully oppress my subjects—and by my action today I want to assure them of this. One could argue that the king concluded that what the cleric did was legitimate vengeance (an extension of the principle, *licitum vim vi repellere*), like the feud—archaic perhaps, but not in itself unlawful. In any case, the onlookers expressed delight in Louis IX's threat. Much of officialdom must have been appalled.

This account in Jean de Joinville's *Vie de saint Louis* occurs separately from his lyrical writing about Louis IX's reform of administration in Paris *after* his return from crusade, which I will now quote at length and in full. You will recall that the king returned from the Holy Land in 1254 after an absence from France of six years.

At that time the office of *prévôt* of Paris used to be sold to the *bourgeois* of the city, or to [some] among them. And so it was that any of these men, having purchased the office, would tolerate the scandalous behaviour (*outrages*) of his children and nephews;

these youths (*jouvenciaus*) could rely on the protection of their parents and friends who held the *prévôté*. The humbler people (*le menu peuple*) were sorely oppressed as a result and could not assert their rights against the rich men because of the lavish presents and gifts the wealthy gave to the *prévôt*. During that time anyone who told the truth to the *prévôt*, or who wanted to uphold an oath so as not to be forsworn in the matter of a debt or anything else he was obliged to answer for, was fined and punished by the *prévôt*. Because of the great injustices and the great robberies committed by the *prévôts*, the humbler people did not dare stay in the king's land; instead they went to live in other *prévôtés* and in other lordships. The king's [land was] so empty that when the *prévôt* held his court no more than ten or twelve people came.

Besides, there were so many criminals and thieves in Paris and beyond that the whole country (*païs*) was full of them. The king, who was very mindful of how the humbler people were being looked after, saw the whole truth. And so he refused to allow the position of *prévôt* of Paris to be sold any more. He gave a generous and substantial salary to those who were to hold the post thereafter and abolished all the bad customs by which the people could be burdened. He made enquiries throughout the region (*pays*) and the kingdom as to where he might find a man who would do good and firm justice, and who would not spare the rich man any more than the poor. He was told about [Étienne] Boileau, who [maintained and kept] the office of *prévôt* so effectively that no criminal, thief or murderer dared remain in Paris; if he did he would be swiftly hanged and no parent or relative or gold or silver could save him. The king's [land] began to improve, and people came to [it] because of the sound justice done there. There was such population growth and regeneration that the king's revenues from land sales, legal proceedings, trade and other sources doubled in value compared with earlier times.[21]

For generations scholars accepted Jean de Joinville's words at more or less face value, especially since the *Grandes Chroniques*, the quasi-official royal history written at the abbey of Saint-Denis, and other chronicles agreed with him.[22] Then in the late nineteenth century Colonel Léon-Louis Borrelli de Serres published a series of studies on early French administration, which were breathtaking in their brilliance, impressive in their creative use of sources, and disagreeable in their pugnacious projection of infallibility.[23] There is a memoir on the colonel in the so-called Archive Dampierre, a privately deposited archive in the Archives Nationales, with restricted access. When it becomes available it may shed light on the personality and motives of this choleric scholar.[24] In any case, Borrelli set out to show in one of his studies that most of Jean de Joinville's talk about the reform of the *prévôté* of Paris was misleading or false or dependent on other sources that were misleading or false. He believed that the old *sénéchal* had borrowed from and had exponentially and unjustifiably expanded the notice in the *Grandes Chroniques*. Things happened—reform was occurring everywhere—but the focus on Étienne Boileau in the narrative sources, Borrelli de Serres insisted, was a complete misrepresentation. He found evidence that there were direct payments of salaries to a few *prévôts* following the king's return from crusade and prior to Étienne Boileau's appointment. Revenue farmers also probably worked with these *prévôts* and, he implied, should not be confused with them. Moreover, the signal production of Étienne's provostship, the statutes of the craft guilds and the guildmen's obligations to the policing of the city, the *Livre des métiers*, Borrelli concluded, contained nothing new. How could such a production properly be assimilated to a major reform? And so on.[25] To the extent that Borrelli de Serres clarified the details of Louis IX's interventions in administrative developments in Paris in the 1250s and 1260s, I incorporated his findings into my own published work long ago, but I was then and remain hesitant

47

to buy into his wholesale dismissal of so much and so many of the narrative sources.[26]

From the prickly colonel in 1895 to the indignant Arié Serper in 1979 was eighty-four years, but merely a single step to kneeling at Borrelli de Serre's altar of skepticism.[27] Jean de Joinville and all like-minded sources, he intoned, were deceivers. How could a man, the late Professor Serper implied, or a copyist of Jean's book who got his information from the *Grandes Chroniques* written by the monks of Saint-Denis a quarter century after the events be trusted? To call what happened as a result of Louis IX's appointment of Étienne Boileau a reform, let alone to characterize the appointment itself as a reform, caused Serper to gag at the very word. In a mere three pages he placed the word reform in quotation marks eight times to underline his thorough-going disgust with its use.[28] Following on this indictment Claude Gauvard has spoken of the alleged reform as stereotype and myth and asserted on the basis of the wispiest of evidence that the allegedly distorted narrative reports were concocted merely to provide a justification for imposing the death penalty for theft, that is, for crimes against property.[29] And so it has gone: Raymond Cazelles called Jean de Joinville's report "deformed."[30]

Boris Bove's long and otherwise valuable study of the *échevinage* of Paris is the most recent to weigh in on these matters. The book affirms almost all, if not quite all, the factual clarifications Borrelli de Serres had offered about the events from 1254 to 1270 in the history of the administration of Paris.[31] Bove was also strident in his dismissal of the narrative sources, for the same reasons Borrelli de Serres and Serper were, namely, that there were substantive aspects of the reforms earlier, the appointment of some reformed officials earlier, and the like. Authors of narrative sources borrowed from—or at least informed—one another and were not wholly independent. There was therefore no genuine cloud of witnesses to the allegedly revolutionary implications of Louis IX's appointment of Étienne Boileau as *prévôt*. And it was only the attractively neat simplicity of fixing on one man, Étienne Boileau, as Louis IX's counterpart that seduced these authors, blinded (Bove's word) by their admiration of Louis IX, into overstating the *prévôt*'s role.[32] Why of any number of men did they focus on Étienne? Possibly, Bove suggested, because he (that is, Étienne Boileau) had assembled and published the customs and regulations of the Paris guilds.[33]

After reading Borrelli de Serres, Serper and Bove, one would think the *sénéchal* of Champagne had never even been to Paris rather than having frequently visited the royal court there. One would think that no one who was still living twenty-five or thirty years after Étienne Boileau's appointment and who had access to the *Grandes Chroniques*, remembered or even could remember Étienne Boileau's administration. Only if this were so, could those devious monkish authors have played as fast and loose with the truth as Borrelli de Serres, Serper and Bove imply that they did in polishing the image of Louis IX to facilitate his canonization. One would think that the man behind the formulation of the *Grandes Chroniques*, Mathieu of Vendôme, the abbot of Saint-Denis, a member of *Parlement*, a man whom the king called upon for sensitive diplomatic and political missions and made co-regent of the kingdom, did not have a clue about how government and administration operated. Or, if he did have a clue, he was nonetheless a consummate liar when he let the king's administration be described as it was in Saint-Denis's chronicles.[34] One would think that the creation of a huge, comprehensive and systematic statement of disparate customs and obligations appertaining to the Parisian craft guilds, the *Livre des métiers*, was just an idea whose time had come (*pace* Bove) and was a fairly easy undertaking (*pace* Serper)—certainly no big deal. And yet, men as learned as Léopold Delisle and Jacques Le Goff have insisted that it was a big deal.[35] Indeed, it was clearly a big enough deal to have made the authors of the narrative sources (again, *pace* Bove) focus on the man,

Étienne Boileau, who assembled the *Livre*—that is to say, to focus on him as the icon of reform.

But perhaps nothing is more galling about Borrelli de Serres's, Serper's, and Bove's representation of events than the assumption that the sources' highlighting of Étienne Boileau's role in the reform (no quotation marks on my part) is incompatible with tentative earlier adjustments, adjustments which, I would argue, Louis IX continued to make after placing the former *prévôt* of Orléans in charge of the administration of Paris.[36] So, while I still accept the fuller details developed by Borrelli de Serres, Serper and Bove and followed now by most scholars, I absolutely and unequivocally reject their dismissive criticism of the narrative sources. Léopold Delisle's gentleness notwithstanding, his criticisms of Borrelli de Serres's work, which run like a red thread through his magisterial essay on the personnel of the French administration, and his own insistence on the key place of Étienne Boileau in Louis IX's reform of the *prévôté* suggest that his views substantially harmonize with my own.[37] Jacques Le Goff's book expresses the same distaste for Borrelli de Serres's "polemic," and Jean Richard's study shows its author's attitude by his reliance on and refusal to indulge in a diatribe against the narrative sources.[38]

So, how does the case of Étienne Boileau now stand or how should it stand? First, Louis IX chose Étienne

Boileau. All the sources and scholars agree on this. Despite Bove's expression of utter bafflement at how this was accomplished,[39] the process whereby *administrative personnel* might have conveyed their preference is not at all hard to imagine. For Jean de Joinville's words used in describing Louis IX's selection of Étienne ("he made enquiries throughout the *pays* and the kingdom"), which is the source of Bove's bafflement, can readily be understood to imply that the king consulted his *baillis*, the men who came to Paris three times a year to render their accounts and to defend any of their judgments against which suitors had appealed to the *Parlement* of Paris.[40] Louis IX would also have consulted his *enquêteurs*. These were men, many of whom were Dominican and Franciscan friars, who periodically toured the provinces holding local inquiries to receive complaints against royal officials, including provincial *prévôts*— complaints and praise, too, that might not otherwise have reached the king's ear.[41] It is also well known that the king routinely kept notes on men who were recommended to him for positions of responsibility and followed up on these recommendations by finding out more about them.[42] He was then prepared to make or, if what he found out was negative, not to make an appointment if a position came open.

The assertion is also made by an anonymous chronicler that the "voice of the people" (*voix du peuple*) was listened to in Étienne Boileau's selection.[43] None of the scenarios I have suggested about Louis IX's consultation of administrative personnel on an appropriate appointee to the *prévôté* of Paris seems quite to describe the voice of the people. Is it just a phrase, an exaggeration, mythography? An alternative explanation seems better to me. The king must have been in touch at least indirectly with many leading merchants, heads of the craft guilds and other worthies of Paris, whose residences and businesses were located in those parts of the city under royal administration. There were many other seigneurial jurisdictions in the city as well.[44] The *bourgeois* were concerned with the situation in the neighborhoods and in the surrounding areas more generally and could discern differences between royally administered neighborhoods and those more efficiently governed and policed under other lords. Not all of the *bourgeois* of Paris could have been of the same mind. Many benefitted from the loose control exercised before the king's reforms, reforms which did in fact begin before the appointment of Étienne Boileau in 1261. Several names came to the king's attention, and he would have—directly or indirectly—sought the input of those *bourgeois*, the voice of the people, who wanted a strengthening of order in their neighborhoods.

Borrelli de Serres, Serper and Bove insistently made the point that Étienne Boileau was preceded by other *prévôts* of Paris who were of a reformist character beginning around 1254. And I have already accepted this as fact, but as I see it, Étienne turned out to be one of the best of the sequence, and Louis IX kept him in office until his (Étienne's) death nearly a decade after his appointment. Let us return briefly to that other story Jean de Joinville told of the cleric who killed three royal sergeants of the *prévôté* of Paris on the eve of the crusade. Two points need to be made. First, the people, bystanders and onlookers, spoke then, praising the king for not punishing a man who took the law into his own hands to avenge himself of an outrage on his body and by extension to protect them from the oppression of local officials who committed violent crimes. This was not the voice of the people calling for the appointment of Étienne Boileau that any chronicler was referring to after the crusade, but it is a voice that could not have been forgotten by the concerned monarch.

Second, when I retold Jean de Joinville's story of the cleric and especially when referring to the then-*prévôt* of Paris's role in it, I did not note that official by name. The events can be securely dated from December 1244, when Louis IX first took the crusader's vow, to June 1248 when he departed Paris. Who was the *prévôt* of Paris in these years? Well, there was Eudes Popin and Raoul de Paci sharing the office in 1245; and then there was Renaud le Conte in 1246. Thereafter,

Gautier le Maître and Guerne de Vèrberie assumed the provostship in 1247. Guerne continued down to 1250, or at least he appears in the position at that date and again in 1253. Eudes Popin, *prévôt* in 1245, and temporarily out of office perhaps, was certainly sharing the office again in 1250.[45] So, to repeat, who was the *prévôt*? This succession would not have been as confusing on the ground as it is to modern scholars. The administration of the *prévôté* may not have suffered and the *prévôts* themselves may have been good men, even *prud'hommes*, but the rapidity of the turnover suggests an ineffective structure of government in Paris, a conclusion, which Cazelles affirmed and which the anecdote of the cleric who killed the three royal sergeants reinforces.[46] Perhaps the burden of proof should rest on those who believe that there was no truly profound reason to reform the administration of Paris.

The problems that the post-crusade reformed *prévôts* faced in the 1250s and that Étienne Boileau faced as *prévôt* of Paris in the 1260s were not necessarily caused by organized or professional criminals, although there must have been a great many of them in a city like Paris—cut purses, burglars, dealers in stolen goods, and the like. Allegedly there was also, before the reforms, malfeasance, which is to say, bribery of some of the unreformed administrators. The sources, like Jean de Joinville's *Vie de saint Louis*, actually provide a taxonomy of the bribery. Some merchants and wealthy craftsmen paid off certain of the old-style administrators in order to obtain favorable judgments when they were charged with fraud. Others did so when they wanted to escape obligations that they could not fulfill and claims brought against them for their failure to fulfill them. As I read it, this is the force of the *sénéchal*'s statement that certain of those who made complaints faced fines or punishment, some form of distraint of persons or goods, for bringing what were rejected as false civil claims. Some of the old-style administrators, so the allegations went, were willing, for a price, to turn a deaf ear to the truth-content of the complaints of those who felt legitimate debts owed to them were not being paid or that goods and services that they had contracted for were not being delivered or perhaps were not of the quality expected. Bribery was the grease that often enough made the administrative machine run against justice.

Asking for and/or taking bribes were lucrative, if dangerous, pursuits. Did they drive honest people away from Paris, as the narrative sources suggest? Just like today, they may have caused any number of craftsmen and merchants to relocate their businesses to neighborhoods deemed safer, neighborhoods that, in medieval Paris, came under other rather better policed jurisdictions. Jean de Joinville and his sources lauded Louis

IX's willingness to suppress bad customs in the neighborhoods of Paris over which he had jurisdiction and which were stimuli of bad behavior (the use of revenue farming was one such custom that provided regular income to the crown but inspired exploitative behavior among the revenue farmers). There is no doubt that sometimes the impulse to reform came from third parties, that is, from other jurisdictional authorities who approached the king to abolish problematic usages. Louis IX could get a little testy, if he believed he was being criticized unfairly, a conversation basically like this: if you think the custom in my land, like revenue farming, say, has lamentable consequences in that it indirectly generates unsavory behavior, you have a similar custom; why do you not suppress it in your jurisdiction? One of the bishops of Paris received this sort of reply, and then had to report back to the king that the cathedral chapter saw a potential loss of legitimate revenue in the abolition of their custom.[47]

In any case, as long as there was a strongly perceived difference between the quality of life in the neighborhoods under various lordships and as long as the royal neighborhoods suffered in the comparison, people, if they could, relocated their businesses and their residences. Perhaps few could. Certainly few artisans with heavy equipment or who needed access to the Seine's water could. Unsurprisingly, the narrative sources mention that only the humbler people (*le menu peuple*) exercised the option. And, in any case, fewer people presumably cared to attend the *prévôt*'s court when it seemed that decisions contrary to fairness were being handed down ("no more than ten or twelve people came," as Jean de Joinville put it). Given the intricate map of jurisdictions in Paris and its environs, however, merely relocating a short distance to a different lordship or avoiding attendance at the *prévôt*'s court were not entirely satisfactory responses to the problems that vulnerable merchants and craftsmen felt. Nor did such actions protect sufficiently against the hooliganism that paid little attention to the complex jurisdictional boundaries that overlay the city's neighborhoods. The narrative sources are explicit that youthful hooligans (*jouvenciaus*) were a central problem, undoubtedly gangs of adolescent boys and young men (*leurs enfans et leur neveus*). The collective memory, to judge by the narrative sources, knew some of these youths as sons of wealthy Parisians including earlier *prévôts*, going through what we might call a violent phase in their lives. It was comparable *mutatis mutandis* to the aggressive and brutal adolescence and young manhood of aristocratic youth, so vividly detailed by Georges Duby.[48] In the urban context of pre-reform Paris youthful miscreants sometimes managed to secure protection from judicial punishment by parents' and relatives' bribery. All of these injustices and the bribery that underlay them were laid before the king who, recalling Jean de Joinville's words, "saw the whole truth," perhaps even the poor attendance at his *prévôt*'s court.

Unlike Robert of Sorbon, Étienne Boileau was not a courtier, although he is referred to as a *prud'homme*.[49] (Not one of Louis IX's courtiers has been identified as bourgeois.)[50] That Étienne was not one is an important point. Being a courtier, as in Robert of Sorbon's case, conferred great prestige on a man and gave him influence. Suggestions from the mouth of Robert of Sorbon may not have been immediately understood by his interlocutors as having the king's backing, but his words were inevitably taken more seriously because of his courtier status. So the first thing for Louis IX and Étienne Boileau to establish when the latter became *prévôt* of Paris was a similar intimacy or the hint that such intimacy, which would bestow prestige on the administrator, existed. Dom Félibien (d. 1719), whose knowledge of the sources of Parisian history was unrivalled and accurate, can help us here. He had access in the late seventeenth and early eighteenth century to sources destroyed in successive wars and in devastating fires, like the fire at the royal treasury in 1737, which virtually wiped out the crown's medieval fiscal accounts. He knew of a report registering contemporary concern about how Étienne Boileau needed to be represented to the Parisian elite and other administrators. He recorded a *récit*, which told how Louis IX deliberately chose to go to the Châtelet, the fortress which housed the *prévôt*'s administrative offices, including the court, the sergeants' quarters, the prison, and the stables. It was no distance from the royal palace to the *prévôt*'s offices in the Châtelet, but those offices, so far as I have been able to determine, were not a site that was, one might say, typically on the monarch's itinerary.

Early on in Étienne Boileau's provostship Louis IX had expended funds to have the Châtelet refurbished and enhanced.[51] The reason the king visited Étienne at his headquarters, according to the report Dom Félibien summarized, was to be in formal attendance on the *prévôt*, literally to sit beside him like a judicial councilor (*asseoir auprès de lui le mesme Boisleau*), and the reason for this was "to encourage him in order to make him an example for other judges of the kingdom" (*pour l'encourager à donner l'exemple aux autres juges du royaume*).[52] Étienne Boileau thereby was not merely at the governmental center of the kingdom by serving in the capital city, he was at the symbolic center, visibly, as the king's *protégé* who sat with the greater man at his side while he was meting out justice. Besides the king, the *prévôt*, the *prévôt*'s judicial councilors, the accused and their accusers, Étienne's assistants would have been at these sessions. In 1264 the assistants included the guards as well as administrative assistants like Jean le Coeur (*Johannes le Cuer*), Étienne's personal clerk, and Simon of Saint-Julien (*Simon de Sancto-Juliano*), the resident clerk of the Châtelet who would have enrolled the *prévôt*'s decisions.[53] I do not know how often the king waited upon Étienne and his court, but it is hardly a stretch of the imagination to suggest that even a few such instances helped demonstrate the *prévôt*'s closeness to the king and his (Étienne's) exalted authority. It was this newly revealed authority that would have attracted observers to his court, far more than the ten or twelve Jean de Joinville lamented, if only to marvel at the king's presence, and emboldened him (Étienne) to act with decision.

And with decision he did act, taking a leading place in the erection of Louis IX's morally repressive regime, a regime whose long range goal was nothing less than the salvation of the kingdom. Hooliganism was a problem. Étienne did not run roughshod over the law. Quite the contrary the royal *prévôt* rigorously though expeditiously adhered to legal forms. He was, as far as one can tell, however, relentless in the imposition of the most draconian punishments that the law permitted. Thus, the narrative sources that have already been summarized note with evident satisfaction that "no criminal, thief or murderer dared remain in Paris; if he did he would be swiftly hanged and no parent or relative or gold or silver could save him." Was this an anti-liberal screed in favor of capital punishment for crimes against property, *pace* Gauvard? Perhaps in part. But note the phrases well. No parent or relative—the implication is that late adolescents and young men who were hooligans were targeted successfully. No gold or silver—the implication is that the culture of bribery was fractured.

There was a cost to all this, and it is revealed almost frighteningly by the chroniclers. Even generally honest men and women might put themselves at risk of punishment by attempting to bribe judges or guards in order to protect their children from capital punishment, for appeals to mercy do not appear to have swayed Étienne Boileau. At the same time, the regime craved legitimacy for the agents of its repressive measures, its rigorous justice. "And, it happened," more than one chronicler notes, "that during this *prévôt*'s term one of his own godsons (*ung sien filleul*)" went astray. This chronicler reports that the godson was beloved of Étienne Boileau (*il aimoyt fort*). But when he was taken as a thief, this young man came under the power of the old man, the *prévôt*, who condemned him and refused to retreat from the severity of the punishment.

The godfather had his godson hung (*il le fist pendre*).[54] Adding to the point that the king's law, as administered by Étienne Boileau, was righteous was the additional note to the effect that the *prévôt*'s condemnation actually followed an admission on the part of his godson's mother. She confessed that her son could not keep himself from stealing (*sa mere li dist qu'il ne se pooit tenir d'embler*).[55]

Empathy is a terribly risky business in writing history, but I believe that this confession begs for it. I do not read it as a chronicler's twisted retelling meant to ally the mother with the rigorous application to her son of capital justice for crimes against property. I see it as a parent's plea that her son simply could not help himself. It is not something that she could understand or would endorse, but the compulsion, she hoped, might itself be taken as exculpation. Yet no excuse obtained Étienne Boileau's mercy. The decision stressed the even-handedness and consistency of Étienne Boileau's and therefore Louis IX's application of justice. For good measure our informant added that on a different occasion, the *prévôt* had an associate (*compere*) of his, the *prévôt*'s, executed by hanging because the latter yielded to the temptation of a stuffed money belt placed in his keeping.[56]

The administrative staff that Étienne could call upon to impose Louis IX's and his kind of justice on those parts of Paris in which he exercised the king's authority depended for its success on policing. I do not wish to go into too much detail, but the *Livre des métiers* was not simply a masterful laying out of mercantile customs and guild regulations, it was also a careful definition of the powers and obligations of the guilds, considered as a municipal corporation. These obligations included providing supplementary police forces, the watch (*guet*). The investigations that preceded the redaction of the *Livre* had identified a host of legitimate exemptions from this service. No attempt was made to turn back the clock, but every effort was made to make sure obligations still in force were carried out. The principle of community responsibility for contributing to policing was never abandoned. The supervisory role for all such matters, that is to say, administrative review, lay with the royal *prévôt*. At the same time we know that the police forces serving directly under the *prévôt* (the *servientes Castelleti*) were augmented in a major way by the crown and the professional character of both the watch and the *prévôt*'s force was enhanced by the appointment of tried administrators who served as captains (*custodes; chevaliers du guet*).[57]

Aggressive policing sometimes led to jurisdictional disputes. It is the evidence of these disputes that persuades me that Étienne Boileau's regime was scrupulous in its respect of legal rules. One Guillaume Broc was keeping a boarding house or hostel of rather ill-repute for some time in Paris in the 1260s.[58] In two separate incidents in 1266 alone, the king's men entered the house to arrest suspects staying there. The alleged crimes were very serious indeed, one a conspiracy against the king, the other a murder.[59] The disposition of the case of the alleged conspiracy is the one I will concentrate on, but both cases demonstrate the jurisdictional restraint exercised by the king and Étienne's administration. Guido Livardi was supposed to have been carrying letters, which were evidence of a plot against the king and certain of his barons (*deferebat secum litteras sedicionis in regem et barones Francie*). The deep background is fairly clear. At the request of Thomas II of Savoy, who was one of the king's brothers, Charles d'Anjou's supporters in Italy and was also at war with the Piedmontese commune of Asti, Louis IX interned and seized the property of a number of Astigians in retaliation for the commune's imprisonment of Thomas following his defeat at the battle of Montebruno in February 1255. There was a significant community of Astigians who owned and operated banking establishments in France. Some fled, before Louis IX's order could be enforced. Those who were interned, having suffered significantly during their incarceration, were released in the early 1260s, probably not until 1265, that is, after a considerable length of time in prison and on the payment of a collective indemnity reputed to be 30,000 pounds. The Astigian chronicle of Ogerio Alfieri gives the number of interned Astigians as one hundred fifty, specifies the length of their interment as six years or more, and characterizes their incarceration as painful.[60] These assertions have been accepted in the standard scholarship.[61]

Resentment necessarily ran high against the French king. Guido Livardi who was undoubtedly a member of this Astigian community had decided to act on this resentment after the release in 1265 or was suspected of deciding to.[62] But it was demonstrated over the course of time during which Guido was being held in royal custody at the Châtelet for the reputed plot that the boarding house from which he was taken actually lay within the boundary of a neighborhood under the jurisdiction of the abbey of Sainte-Geneviève. When this was made clear as a consequence of an investigation by men of probity (*habito bonorum consilio*), Louis IX relented. He had Étienne Boileau send two knights and two royal sergeants to deliver the captive to the abbey prison. The alleged murderer in the other case I have alluded to was also handed over to the abbey officials at the king's command (*de mandato regis, nobis deliberatus fuit*). And as a matter of fact, Guido's trial in the abbey's court led to his acquittal and the murder case ended in an arbitrated settlement. The acquittal may have gagged in the king's and *prévôt*'s throats, but if so, no counteraction was undertaken.

Let us return to the narrative sources once more. Did life in Paris really improve to the extent that people who had left royal neighborhoods came back? Perhaps a number of houses of ill-repute, similar to Guillaume Broc's hostelry, were targeted and shuttered. Some legitimate merchants and craftsmen may have reopened closed shops. Equally or perhaps more likely is that existing shops and workplaces expanded, and under-inhabited housing attracted reputable tenants. If this was so, and I believe it was, then it is not a stretch to imagine neighbors and visitors sensing a real growth in the community of residents and experiencing an increase in rents, in payments for land and building conveyancing, in taxes on sales in markets, and in fees from the registering of debts and contracts, as the *sénéchal* of Champagne remarks. Were revenues doubled *solely* as a result of these developments, as Jean de Joinville also states? Of course this is hyperbole. However the reforms played their role in an otherwise favorable economic climate in the mid-thirteenth century that saw considerable and steady growth in the population and the gross domestic product in Paris and in France more generally.[63]

Right up until the end of his life, Étienne Boileau fought his master's battles as best he could. Increasingly it was less a question of rampant crime—and it was never a question of bribery of officials under his regime—than a question of making sure jurisdictional boundaries were respected among the myriad of rights holders in Paris. The canons of the cathedral chapter of Notre-Dame, like most large ecclesiastical corporations, kept good records and were zealous in the defense of their liberties and jurisdiction. In December 1269 Étienne's challenge to a liberty claimed by the canons provoked a spirited response from them.[64] In anger they excommunicated the *prévôt*. It was a complicated situation, but like many kings Louis IX had worked steadily to get papal endorsement of the view that his officials could not be excommunicated without his permission. The point was that governance would be compromised if the king's subjects had to cut off contact with the excommunicated royal officials.[65] So, Louis intervened.

The king did not send Robert of Sorbon, who was a canon there. Doing so would have produced a conflict of interest. Instead, he chose Philippe of Cahors, another *clerc du roi*, to negotiate with the canons. Philippe had just become or was about to become bishop of Evreux, to which Mathieu of Vendôme, the abbot of Saint-Denis and future co-regent, had declined appointment. Philippe's credentials, at least by association, were even stronger than this suggests. He had served as an *enquêteur* on a two-man panel in 1258, a panel whose other member was Louis IX's close friend Gui Foucois, who not long afterward left the royal administration for the church, rising rapidly to become Pope Clement IV (1264-1268). Philippe of Cahors was an interesting man, on whom unfortunately, as Léopold Delisle lamented long ago, there is still no first-rate biographical notice.[66]

All the parties to the dispute, the excommunicated Étienne Boileau and the canons of Notre-Dame, as well as the king's delegate Philippe of Cahors, came to an agreement on the nature of the privilege claimed by the canons. Philippe promised that the canons would receive satisfaction. In return they agreed to end the confrontation with a solemn ceremony celebrated on Christmas Day 1269. Then it was that Étienne Boileau's absolution and the lifting of his excommunication were pronounced.[67] He died soon after, certainly by April 1270 when his successor was in office. A charter that mentions the former *prévôt*'s daughter as the child of the late Étienne Boileau assures us on this point. The charter is the one noted at the beginning of this chapter which also refers to him as a knight.[68] It is barely possible that the *prévôt* did come of an impoverished knightly family but had put off being dubbed in early manhood because he lacked the fortune to pursue the knightly life. (Such choices have been documented

69

in other cases.[69]) Since he was not ennobled in a formal sense, formal ennoblement being a somewhat later phenomenon,[70] the only other possibility and indeed the only likely one is that suggested by Raymond Cazelles, who concluded that the title was a courtesy.[71] Support for Cazelles's opinion is the fact that in the last years of Étienne's provostship, his administrative status was assimilated to that of the *baillis*, who were in fact knights; Étienne himself was being referred to interchangeably as *prévôt* of Paris and *bailli* of the city.[72] And Gérard Sivéry in his published work actually came to prefer and to adopt the usage *prévôt-bailli* to denominate Étienne's office.[73]

To come to an end: Étienne Boileau represented in the administration of Paris the same vision—the same unforgiving vision, it must be said—of a disciplined society that his king's governance everywhere and at all times conveyed. The deliberate performance of justice with the king by his own decision in attendance at the Châtelet made it impossible to avoid the impression of a shared vision between king and administrator for anyone who cared to think about it. The career of a third man at the center of governance, the man who is the subject of Chapter Three, Simon de Nesle, allows us to see this shared vision translated into action by a member of the high aristocracy.

Chapter Three

Simon de Nesle, Aristocrat

In his maturity the man known to historians as Simon de Nesle was a truly lofty aristocrat, connected by marriage to one of France's greatest families, and a lord of enormous wealth and prestige. Yet, at the time of his birth about the year 1209, there was no expectation that Simon himself would succeed to the principal cluster of family properties, the lordship of Ailly-sur-Noye, which his father Raoul held. Indeed, when his father died, it was Simon's elder brother, Jean, who inherited. The childless Jean, however, predeceased Simon, and the seigneurie of Ailly passed to the latter. And then in 1239 another opportune death, that of his uncle, also without issue, enhanced Simon's holdings through his inheritance of the lordship of Nesle.[1] Simon's marriage to Alix, Amaury de Montfort's daughter, was another factor in his prestige.[2] Amaury de Montfort, as is well known among historians, was the son of Simon de Montfort, the baronial commander in the early phases of the Albigensian Crusade (1209–1229). The early phases of the Crusade had seen Simon de Montfort conquer a vast territory in southern France and assume the titles and lands of several of the vanquished nobles, most significantly those of the count of Toulouse. The middle years of the Crusade were less happy ones for the house of Montfort. Successful nativist resurgence against the northerners, Simon de Montfort's death in 1218 at the siege of Toulouse, which had been intended to retake the city, and Amaury's inability to hold onto many of the territories thereafter inspired the latter to cede his lineage's claims to Languedoc to the French crown.[3] In partial recompense later on, Amaury assumed the honorific office of constable of France.[4] Simon de Nesle's marital union with Alix de Montfort therefore allied him with a noble family of almost mythic significance in the history of the French monarchy.

The principal material base for Lord Simon's career, the lordship of Nesle in Picardy, was also impressive. Nesle itself began life as a small fortified settlement, but by the thirteenth century it possessed, besides the castle chapel, a collegiate church dedicated to the Virgin, serving four parishes, a hospital, and a leprosarium. At least sixty other villages made up the Nesle lordship, whose agricultural lands were notable for their productivity. Additionally the family drew considerable income from the tolls that had devolved on it from the crown and were generated along the (formally) royal road that ran through the heart of the seigneurie. We know of the extent of these tolls partly through the exemptions from them enjoyed by Cistercian houses, whose charters denote and describe them.[5]

Given the geographical placement of the family holdings, the Nesle lineage might have leaned either toward the Flemish and their English allies or toward the French in the long-running political and military conflicts between these parties.[6] But early on the family cast its lot with the French side and maintained its fidelity.[7] The uncle from whom Simon inherited the seigneurie of Nesle had fought in support of the French against the Flemish and German allies of the English at the Battle of Bouvines in 1214, the battle, which in the retelling over centuries, was said to have made France.[8] The same uncle also fought with Louis VIII in the later phases of the Albigensian Crusade, when that king, Louis IX's father, endeavored in an impressive military cavalcade to make the crown's claims to the Montfort conquests a reality. Indeed Lord Jean de Nesle, our Simon's uncle, was present in Montpensier in the Auvergne at the end of the royal campaign when Louis VIII took to his sick bed. In the presence of the weak and fading king Lord Jean promised fealty to the new king, the boy of twelve who was far away in Paris and under his mother Blanche of Castile's tutelage, if the situation should come to that—as it did when Louis VIII died soon after.[9]

Until his own death in 1239, Simon's uncle continued to serve the royal family, thus laying the foundation for his nephew's close relations with Blanche of Castile and Louis IX. He and his wife dwelt in Paris most of the time, only giving up the sumptuous residence they had built toward the end of his life. The recipient of the gift of the residence was the queen mother, Blanche of Castile. This closeness with Blanche, which the gift implies, underscores why she employed Simon's uncle earlier on another delicate task. He was a member of the delegation that was sent south to Provence to make the final arrangements for Louis IX's marriage to Marguerite of Provence and to convey her northward to Sens for the ceremony.[10] In brief, the Nesle family never deviated from its loyalty and willingness to serve the Capetians. When Simon acceded to the lordship in 1239, most observers would have assumed that this close fruitful relationship would continue. It did. In fact, it deepened.

I will call Simon, the focus of this chapter, Simon de Nesle. In fact he had an array of titles because of the array of properties that he held: many charters refer to him as *dominus* Simon, let us say, Sir Simon, *miles* or *chevalier* de Nesle, but others add or substitute de Clermont, d'Ailly-sur-Noye, and de Beaulieu, another property he held. Far in the future, the lineage picked up even loftier titles, like marquis in 1545, but later genealogists, in error, read the loftier title back in time, asserting that Lord Simon de Nesle was also the marquis de Nesle.[11] The truth is, Simon did have other titles which were impressive—informally but critically important was that of courtier and formally and even more exalted, was regent of France, a title he bore twice. We will get to his regencies later. Now let us look at his career as a courtier in the ambit of Louis IX.

It is fairly clear that Simon's success in attaching himself to Louis IX's court received encouragement from Queen Blanche. The youthful *rico hombre*, Afonso of Portugal, was one of the queen-mother's nephews, and insofar as one can tell, she liked him a great deal. In an act concerning him issued in November of 1241, Simon acted as a guarantor.[12] He would not have been asked to do so if he did not command the queen-mother's trust and probably her affection as well. It is not surprising then that when Louis IX went on crusade and Simon stayed in France, one of his services was to act as an adviser to Blanche of Castile, who assumed the regency in her son's absence.[13] As a result Simon saw firsthand and up close how government was run at the very center and learned valuable lessons, which came in handy later in his career as a regent himself.

The issues the country faced during the king's absence on crusade in the 1250s were not trivial, including as they did an uprising known as the Crusade of the Shepherds in the spring and early summer of 1251. The expressed purpose of the leaders of this movement was to rescue the king who had been captured in the Egyptian campaign. Blanche was initially hesitant to suppress the Shepherds (actually an amalgam of rural and urban laborers)—men who expressed such fidelity to her son—but she changed her mind in the face of the anti-aristocratic, anti-clerical and anti-Jewish violence that increasingly characterized their movement.[14] Another issue that arose in the regency was that of ecclesiastical favoritism in the government after Queen Blanche's death in November 1252. The regency council that was constituted for the king's ten-year-old son following his grandmother's passing was comprised exclusively, it seems, of prelates.[15] I suspect that Simon de Nesle recognized this as bad policy and later, after Louis IX's return from crusade, persuasively made his views known to the king.

Simon de Nesle's role as an adviser may have diminished with the creation of the regency council, but he continued to offer his services in defense of the crown. One of the most important problems arose from the violation of an agreement that Louis IX had brokered before he left between the Dampierre and the Avesnes families, families which had, in each case, a disputed claim to the counties of Flanders and Hainaut. During Louis IX's absence, the agreement broke down. The Avesnes, who were never very happy with it, seized on an incident in 1251 to renounce it and, more, to over-turn it. The leader of the Avesnes faction put troops into the field. The French blamed him for doing so but obviously looked with trepidation at the specter of war as the Dampierres also raised an army. This was a de-velopment that could only hinder efforts to resupply the king who had chosen to stay in the Holy Land af-ter his release from captivity. Blanche was initially hes-itant to let her son Charles d'Anjou—recently returned from crusade where he, too, had been ransomed—get involved. She wanted him and his brother Alphonse de Poitiers to return to the Holy Land to help Louis IX. Alphonse was ill, and Charles was too tempted by the nearer opportunities offered by the strife in Flanders and Hainaut. Ultimately, after Blanche's death, a major French force was dispatched to support the Dampierre troops, but this force was defeated on the 4th of July 1253 at West-Capelle in Zeeland. Simon de Nesle was among the commanders taken prisoner.[16] The situation improved when Charles d'Anjou counterattacked and a sort of stalemate was achieved. But the old arbitrated judgment was only fully reimposed after Louis IX's return from crusade.[17] The point is that Simon de Nesle like his whole lineage again demonstrated his loyalty to the Capetians. The aristocracy's volatility was also brought home to him in the events he lived through, which was good preparation for his own future service to the crown.

In the circumstances personal relations between the great aristocrat and the king grew warmer. Louis Carolus-Barré, one of the greatest experts on the reign of Louis IX—the twentieth-century scholar who knew the royal *acta* best—may have waxed too admiring when he asserted that Simon from 1257 onward was present on every significant occasion during the last dozen years or so of Louis IX's rule.[18] But the lord of Nesle was certainly in attendance at many. He accompanied the king to the translation of the relics of Saints Quentin, Victorinus, and Cassian which took place at Saint-Quentin on the 2nd of September 1257. Louis IX loved to attend *translationes* of saints' bodies from one grave or reliquary to another, more honorable or sumptuous. He used the occasions to ignite enthusiasm for the crown and its various self-imposed missions, including representing France as a holy realm devoted to the saints.[19]

Simon had significant roles to play in the events surrounding the two most important treaties negotiated in Louis IX's mature years, the Treaty of Corbeil of 1258 and the Treaty of Paris of 1259. The Treaty of Corbeil defined the boundary between France and Aragon and thereby eliminated a possible *casus belli* based on unresolved jurisdictional disputes in the Pyrenees and on either side of the mountain range, including in Montpellier, the patrimony of the Aragonese ruling house. Simon was present at the sealing of the treaty. And he also attended the marriage of Louis IX's heir, the future Philip III, when he wed Isabella of Aragon in Clermont-Ferrand. The marriage symbolically bound the two kingdoms, France and the Crown of Aragon, together.[20]

The Treaty of Paris dealt with the state of war that technically existed between England and France beginning in 1202, when King Philip II Augustus declared King John of England's fiefs in France forfeit because of the latter's refusal to be adjudicated in the French High Court. John had dishonored a baron, the count of La Marche, by robbing him of his would-be bride and marrying her himself. Eventually the count appealed to King Philip as their mutual overlord to rectify the situation, and Philip in turn summoned the English king not as king but as baron of the fiefs he held of the French crown. John ignored the summons. He did not believe that he could separate his English regality from his status as a French baron and accept trial as a vassal, without in fact compromising his regality. War broke out. By the end of 1204 Philip Augustus conquered Normandy, and other conquests followed in the two decades to come. The most dangerous year for the French during the wars that brought about these conquests was 1214, but after Philip defeated John's Flemish and German allies at Bouvines, which was alluded to earlier, and after his son harassed the English king's forces in the western part of the country at the same time, sending them scurrying back to England, long-term victory was sealed. There were occasional battles and many more threats in the years to come, but over time the war between England and France became colder and colder.[21]

With the original antagonists, John and Philip Augustus, long dead, with the two kings ruling in England and France in the middle decades of the thirteenth century, Louis IX and Henry III, having married sisters of Provence and become friends themselves, the time seemed ripe to end the war, if they could find the appropriate formulas for both sides to save face. They found those formulas through arduous negotiations, and at the end of May 1258 a draft version of the treaty was submitted to representatives of the barons for approval. Simon de Nesle was one of the two French representatives. The two kings formally ratified the treaty in a great ceremony in 1259.[22] The treaty was shadowed, of course, by the English baronage's seizure of power from Henry III in England which, as long as it lasted, was of acute concern to Louis IX. Again one can observe him turning to Simon de Nesle to deal with sensitive matters related to this issue.[23]

A number of other events or incidents provoked the king to turn to Simon de Nesle. What they show is that the two men shared, as Étienne Boileau also shared, an extraordinary understanding of how justice should be meted out. Indeed, Simon was the aristocratic version of Étienne Boileau, whose judicial severity deeply appealed to Louis IX. One case that demonstrates this quite clearly involved the noble lady (*domina*) of the lordship of Pierrelaye. She was accused of arranging her husband's murder. The perpetrator was her lover. The moralizing *récit* of this case, found in testimony that was intended to promote the canonization of Louis IX, stigmatizes the adulterous love at its heart as 'bad love.' The added detail that has most titillated later students is the *domina*'s complicity in disposing of her husband's body by having it thrown into a privy, which we must imagine as a deep covered and foul pit.[24]

After the noblewoman's actions were discovered and royal sergeants arrested her, she broke down. She acknowledged the enormity and horror of her crime in true shame or in a desperate attempt to save her life or in both. That is, she repented of her evil, one might say, trusting or hoping that her evident or pretended contrition would evoke mercy from her judges. The king, as ultimate judge and the man in whom the pardoning power rested, was unimpressed by reports of her contrition. But what is perhaps most surprising is the campaign that was waged on the *domina*'s behalf. She was well connected, of course, being from one of the most distinguished aristocratic families in the area around Pontoise, and those who accepted her contrition as genuine appealed to the king to show her some mercy. One is not talking here merely about provincial nobles making this plea. It may have begun with them, but they successfully enlisted a large number of influential women in the campaign, including the countess of Poitiers, who was the countess of Toulouse in her own right and also, and more significantly, one of Louis IX's sisters-in-law. They also persuaded Marguerite of Provence, the king's own wife, to intervene on the *domina* of Pierrelaye's behalf. Literally practicing what they preached, which is to say, penance and forgiveness, several mendicant friars, both Franciscans and Dominicans, also appealed directly to the king to spare the lady's life.

Another concern also motivated the *domina*'s party. They were sensitive to the shame—the dishonor—of a public execution in the sight of lower class people. Recognizing that the king was disposed to proceed with the execution, they pleaded with him at the very least not to make a public spectacle of her, presumably because it would be inappropriate for a woman to be treated in this way and also because the combination of her sex and her rank ought to guarantee some such privilege. The *récit* as it has come down to us hints that the king was concerned to represent his views as those shared by other men who were wise in the ways of justice. Faced with the pleas for a closed execution, he consulted Simon de Nesle. Simon, in the *récit*, is said to have been a sage on such matters. This is not evidence that he was widely regarded this way in fact. It is evidence, however, that Louis IX represented him to the *domina*'s supporters as a man whose opinion would be objective, governed not by uncontrolled emotion but by temperance, and just— in a word, wise. Nor do I think Louis IX ever imagined that Simon would disagree with him, and the lord of Nesle did not disappoint. Here I dissent from Jean Richard's view that Louis IX out of genuine perplexity turned to Simon de Nesle for advice.[25] However that may be, justice publicly administered, the nobleman insisted, was the best justice. Confirmed in his own opinion, which I do not think he ever doubted, Louis IX ordered the lady of Pierrelaye executed by burning at the castle of Pontoise where the crowds could observe her end.[26]

This was, as suggested, not an isolated instance of the unbending rigor of either Simon's or Louis IX's views. Let us pursue the question of public displays—the performance—of justice. In his own lordship, Simon de Nesle had capital justice. One of the lesser nobles in the seigneurie regularly indulged his appetite for criminal acts. His close relatives, vassals of Lord Simon, could not prevail on their kinsman to restrain himself, and they worried as to the outcome. In the event, he was arrested and convicted for a series of felonies and received Simon's condemnation to death. The kinsmen of the condemned man appealed for a private execution, explicitly to save their lineage from the shame of the public disgrace of one of their line. Simon held firm. It was this story that the lord of Nesle related to the king to certify his support for Louis IX's adamantine hardness toward the lady of Pierrelaye. Public justice—justice performed before the people—was truly exemplary justice, he insisted.[27] As important as social rank was in this society in general, it was irrelevant as far as Louis IX and Simon de Nesle were concerned when crimes were as savage and unnatural as that of the lady of Pierrelaye's or as heinous (vicious, repeated and unrestrained) as in the case Simon was pleased to have adjudicated in his own fief.

If high rank was incapable of mitigating the severity of royal justice or of Simon's, so too was loyal service. When a woman complained that one of the king's men, who was employed in the royal kitchen, had broken into her home and raped her and the accusation reached the king, Louis IX called together the councilors who were present, including Simon de Nesle, and constituted them a court of inquiry. They brought the man and the woman before them to confront each other. He admitted that he had had sex with her, but he slurred her as a prostitute, "a foolish common woman," implying sex was consensual and purchased, certainly not rape. One does not know how, but the woman proved that the king's servant and some accomplices had in fact broken into her home and raped her. The court, being convinced, had no reluctance in condemning the king's man to death, but some of the judges argued that the sentence should be commuted. The point was made, after all. Men would know that the cluster of crimes—housebreaking, rape and lying about them (perjury)—was *liable* to the death penalty even if it was not carried out, as they hoped, in this case. They expressed the opinion that the condemned man's otherwise good service to the king, service to Louis IX, should count for something, should count enough for a reprieve from the execution of the capital sentence. Louis IX rejected the appeal. He seemed to feel that the servant's crime sullied the royal establishment and needed the expiation that would come from the man's execution. The king turned to the man on the court of judgment whom he perhaps trusted most on the matter and who also agreed with him, Simon de Nesle, directing him to make sure that the execution, this time by hanging, was carried out—and he did so.[28]

The death penalty was not appropriate for the outrage that Lord Enguerrand de Coucy committed, the summary executions he inflicted on three young aristocratic Flemish boys who had been playing at hunting in his woods. Enguerrand claimed that he was doing justice. Louis IX, following an investigation into the matter, thought otherwise, arrested the lord of Coucy and imposed a series of crushing fines and obligations on him, sufficient in the short run, though the family recovered, to bankrupt him. Executing him may actually have been urged on Louis, but he resisted the impulse, seeing a difference between the premeditated murder that brought the lady of Pierrelaye to the pyre and the rape and perjury, which delivered his servant to the hangman. What Enguerrand did was an excess, a terrible excess, the investigators concluded, that clearly compromised the lord's right to exercise high justice in his fief. (He was stripped of it.) Expiation, in this case, was supposed to come by the baron's taking the cross and going on crusade. Only by paying a crushing redemption payment, did he avoid this penance, but he was still obliged to endow a memorial chapel and altars in the dead boys' memory.[29]

According to the narrative sources, some barons murmured that bankruptcy and the revocation of seigneurial rights and privileges of this kind and on this scale were themselves excesses that potentially threatened their class as a whole. In Chapter One it was noted that a poet made a similar charge about Louis IX's policies toward the nobility in a song that, arguably, laid part of the blame on Robert of Sorbon. Simon de Nesle, albeit an aristocrat, did not see the situation as Enguerrand's baronial supporters did. He was in fact one of the principal investigators in the Coucy outrage, along with Mathieu of Vendôme, the abbot of Saint-Denis.[30] The punishment of the noble stood.

Simon and Mathieu worked side by side in the Enguerrand de Coucy investigation and got along well together. While representing in their statuses the lay aristocracy and the clergy, they were for all intents and purposes, and more profoundly, representatives of a specifically royal vision of justice. They made a team whose cooperation and coordination on such a difficult and challenging inquiry pleased the king and would, as we shall observe, influence some of his most crucial later decisions. Yet, of course, much of the evidence of Simon's activities on behalf of the crown, to stay with his career, pertains to far less dramatic incidents than the Coucy affair. He was one of the courtiers chosen to attend the king when in June 1268 Louis IX received the delegation of three canons from the cathedral chapter of Notre-Dame of Paris for permission to elect a new bishop.[31] One need only recall that Robert of Sorbon was a member of this delegation to recognize how intimate and interconnected the king's inner circle was. Simon also represented the king in February 1270 in the negotiations over the dower lands that his (Louis IX's) daughter Marguerite was to enjoy when she married Jean de Brabant.[32] The lord of Nesle was frequently present in sessions of *Parlement* from 1254 to 1270 both as a suitor, helping to make judgments, and as a litigant defending his own vast properties and rights.[33] These properties and rights inevitably generated disputes over their limits and precise nature. Such disputes occurred especially with monasteries. In Simon's case he would have had recourse to judgments, arbitrations, investigations and the like, all of which took place in *Parlement*.[34] The occasion for these disputes was whenever charters of donation imprecisely or insufficiently described the endowments they bestowed. More important to our story, when Simon sat in *Parlement*, he had multiple occasions to work, under the eyes of the king, with another frequent suitor, investigator and litigant, Mathieu of Vendôme, the abbot of Saint-Denis.[35]

It was from his inner circle that Louis IX chose Abbot Mathieu of Vendôme and Lord Simon de Nesle to serve as co-regents when he decided to go on crusade a second time.[36] In the lead up to this co-regency Simon appears to have aided in planning the new crusade, probably with the initial expectation of accompanying the king.[37] Because I have written extensively on Abbot Mathieu in a recently published work, I will confine most of my remarks here to his aristocratic and lay counterpart.[38] But with regard to Mathieu let me point out at least in passing that he, like Robert of Sorbon and so many other of the clerical courtiers of Louis IX, was low born.[39] Of course, his later panegyrists, also like Robert's, fabricated a noble origin for him as a kinsman of the counts of Vendôme, but none of that is true.[40] Simon, however, was the real thing, and his selection benefitted the king in two ways. Most significantly, he was secure in his attachment to Louis IX's ideals of governance. Almost as important, the nobility could look to Simon de Nesle as articulating their interests during the period of the regency, which, after all, no one knew was going to be far shorter than the six years of Louis IX's first crusade, when the clerical interest had greater influence. It may seem strange to assert this, since I have depicted Simon as willing to urge punishment of and indeed to severely punish individual aristocrats who acted in ways that challenged the king's understanding of appropriate behavior. Of course, there must have been certain aristocrats who, for these very reasons, were disappointed with Simon's selection as co-regent. Nonetheless, the vast majority of nobles in the country never had direct conflicts with the lord of Nesle, and they knew of him or had heard of him rather as a rich man, a courageous man, the head of a distinguished lineage, and a defender of France. Some indeed may even have admired the way he contributed to disciplining the occasionally errant and arrogant noble of their class, like an Enguerrand de Coucy.

The regency, as noted, was relatively short. Louis IX left Paris in early 1270 and France, from the port of Aigues-Mortes, on the 2nd of July. As an indication of his deeply troubling apprehension (would God let him be defeated again, because of his sins?[41]), he wrote to Simon de Nesle and Mathieu of Vendôme to take particular care to maintain the moral purity of the realm—stressing the repression of prostitution and blasphemy.[42] The obsession with blasphemy, using God's name or the Virgin Mary's for nothing, taking their names in vain, and the determination to rid the realm of it had led the king to authorize draconian punishments for the foul-mouthed. Jean de Joinville clearly found this unsettling. He was not opposed to punishing blasphemers. He affirmed that at Joinville, his estate, "anyone who says these things," by which he meant cursing in the name of the devil, "earns himself a slap on the face or on the hand." Such punishments he believed had nearly wiped out cursing at Joinville.[43]

But the stakes were higher for Louis IX and thus the punishments more degrading. "The king so loved God and his sweet mother that he severely punished all those he could ascertain had spoken basely of them or had sworn blasphemous oaths. I [Jean de Joinville is speaking of himself] saw that he had a goldsmith put in the stocks at Caesarea [while on crusade]. He was wearing his breeches and his chemise and had the guts and innards of a pig piled round his neck—there was such a quantity that it came right up to his nose." And, then Jean added, carefully distinguishing what he had seen from what he had learned from other sources, like the *Grandes Chroniques*, "I heard it said that after my return from overseas he had the nose and lips of one Parisian *bourgeois* branded, although I did not see this myself. And the saintly king said that he would willingly be branded with a hot iron if it would mean his kingdom was rid of all foul oaths."[44] Jean de Joinville's formulation reads to me like special pleading. The king's harshness, branding on the lips and nose, contrasts with the *sénéchal*'s moderation, a slap on the face or on the hand. And yet, he tries to justify Louis IX's behavior by the latter's expressed willingness to be branded himself—as if there was ever any danger of this.

Branding was a fairly common method of treating confessed criminals in thirteenth-century France, particularly those who were banished. Such criminals were branded not on their lips or noses but on their shoulders with a *fleur-de-lysé* iron. The royal fiscal accounts record purchases of the branding irons.[45] The lily (*fleur-de-lys*) marked the criminal as the recipient of French mercy, for banishment was a punishment commonly meted out in lieu of dismemberment or execution. It was meant to prevent the felon from receiving mercy a second time for the commission of a felony, since it identified him or her as a former recipient of the grace, and such grace was typically available only once. Easily covered, the branding mark was not intended to prevent the felon from finding honest work in whatever land of exile he or she took up residence.[46] In the case of blasphemy, assuming that what Jean de Joinville knew indirectly really happened, the mark on the nose and lips had a quite different intent. It publicly announced the humiliation of the blasphemer in the disfigured face, much as the cropping of a thief's ear was intended to stigmatize and as public executions were meant to terrorize into moral behavior. More than this, however, the *fleur-de-lys* as the lily was also a Marian symbol. Mary herself, as it were, wrote her displeasure in the burned flesh of the blasphemer's face. The Virgin's scribe, we should recall, would have been a jailer of the Châtelet, carrying out orders communicated to him by his master Étienne Boileau. For this unfortunate foul-mouthed man was a Parisian bourgeois.

Perhaps it is here in the narrative, while the king has embarked on the voyage that will bring him to the end of his life, leaving Simon de Nesle and Mathieu of Vendôme to execute a last great purification of the realm before the war commences, that one should re-introduce the Marial song *L'autrier matin el moys de may* discussed in Chapter One. Let us recall that it was said to have been the song circulating in the king's court as a kind of inspiration to lovers of profane songs to abandon them and to rededicate their composing, their singing and their hearing to heavenly, salvific, themes—to commend all their artful singing and composing to the service of spiritual enchantment. The very artful nature of the song, with its alternating lines of chivalric French and devotional Latin, cried out for a marriage of liturgy and *trouvère* cleverness in future songs. I would suggest that *L'autrier matin el moys de may* can be understood as the positive side of the branding with the *fleur-de-lysé* iron and the humiliating with pig viscera—the brutal punishments—Louis IX favored for blasphemy. This is not entirely a guess. The section of the only manuscript in which the song meant to displace bawdy sings is found is devoted to explicating the *fleur-de-lys*.[47] And no scholar seems to know why this is so, except to suggest the generic linking of Mary and the lily, but the matter perhaps deserves a little further investigation. One thing is certain: Louis IX understood the *fleur-de-lys* as a device approaching in virtue a sacramental sign.[48]

Let us now return to the narrative. After a brief stay in Sardinia, Louis IX made for Tunisia where he disembarked on the 18th of July. A little more than a month later, on August 25th, the fifty-six year old king died during the siege of Tunis. His successor, Philip III, who had accompanied his father sent word back to France to confirm the offices of the co-regents, but by the spring of 1271 he had returned to France, bringing the regency effectively to an end.[49] The kingdom had been without a king on its soil only about nine months. Yet, it was clear that the old ways were beginning to fade after power passed to Philip III.

The former co-regents and any number of Louis IX's courtiers and servitors were in effect de-centered. Despite an occasional appearance in *Parlement* Simon almost vanishes from the central government's documentary records in the first seven years of Philip III's reign.[50] Nonetheless, as long as they lived, the former king's loyalists remained important personages in their own right, and at times they were consulted on matters on which they had recognized expertise. When circumstances, for example, combined to overwhelm Philip III, particularly when a number of aristocrats turned violently against his favorite Pierre de la Broce, it was men from his father's former inner circle whom he called upon to get at the truth of matters. Thus, Mathieu of Vendôme was employed as the principal investigator of some rumors of a plot against the royal family that may or may not have involved Pierre de la Broce or Philip's second wife.[51] Simon de Nesle, too, reemerged as the favorite declined.[52] When relations between France and Aragon degenerated in the early 1280s over Aragonese policy toward the rule of Philip's Angevin relatives in Sicily, it was Mathieu of Vendôme and Simon de Nesle whom the king consulted, though he showed less restraint than Mathieu—and possibly Simon—originally urged on him.[53] And why not? Philip was a young man. These were old men.

Old men die. And these began to die off. Étienne Boileau passed away around the time Louis IX left Paris on his last crusade in the spring of 1270. Robert of Sorbon died in 1274. Mathieu and Simon lived through the decade of the 1270s. Mathieu had Saint-Denis and the myriad aspects of its administration to occupy him, and Simon had his seigneurie, although as in the reign of Louis IX he continued to live in Paris with only occasional trips to his fiefs in Picardy.[54] Both men testified at the canonization hearings on Louis IX in the summer of 1282 held at the abbey of Saint-Denis.[55] But mortality was staring at least Simon in the face. He had lost his wife a little before October of 1279. She was buried in the Cistercian abbey of Beaupré in Picardy.[56] Simon chose this site for his own burial, unless, he explained in his will, he were to find his end *outre-mer*.[57] Like the man he served, Simon envisioned the crusade as a desirable culmination of his life. In the event, he was denied this opportunity. There was another crusade, but it was not against Muslim powers in North Africa, Egypt or the Holy Land.

Philip III committed his military forces to an invasion of Aragon as retribution for its intervention in Sicily against his uncle Charles d'Anjou, Louis IX's youngest brother. Because papal policy was staunchly pro-Angevin at the time, the Aragonese position was vilified as virtually an act of faithlessness. The French invasion was authorized as a crusade, and in 1285 the invasion, the ill-starred Crusade Against Aragon, began. Before this, however, in a remarkable reenactment of past history, Philip III chose the regents who would rule the kingdom in his absence. He could think of no one better than the two men his father Louis IX had chosen fifteen years before, Mathieu of Vendôme and

Simon de Nesle. Mathieu was the younger man at sixty-three; Simon was seventy-six, and I suspect already in his last illness.[58]

This regency was also brief. Philip III departed Paris in April 1285. He lay dead of disease in the Pyrenees on the 5th of October and there was a new king, his son Philip IV the Fair, to bring his body back to the royal necropolis of Saint-Denis.[59] A few months later Abbot Mathieu and Lord Simon were again doing what they had been doing before their second co-regency, administering Saint-Denis and, if the latter was not too ill, ruling the *seigneurie* of Nesle from Paris respectively.[60] Within months of each other, however, Simon on the 1st of February 1286 and Mathieu on the 25th of September of the same year were dead.[61] Simon's last will and testament reveals in extraordinary detail the extent of his charity.[62] It is germane here because besides the religious establishments in the seigneurie of Nesle on which the lord's largesse might be expected to be bestowed, bestowed lavishly in the extreme here,[63] a number of Parisian institutions beloved of Simon's old master Louis IX received bequests. These included the Dominican and Franciscan friaries of Paris and the house also in Paris of the Friars of the Sack, a convent of one of the minor mendicant orders, of which Louis IX had been the chief supporter in Europe.[64] Simon's wife had earlier left bequests to the same institutions.[65]

He had named as his principal executor another of the old king's courtiers, the "religious and honorable man, my dear friend Mathieu, by the grace of God abbot of Saint-Denis."[66]

One last fact: in 1291 King Philip IV the Fair launched a campaign against the endowment of churches with lands under the regime of mortmain, which is to say, churches were henceforward forbidden to acquire any landed property that might lead to the exemption of that property from dues and services it would have incurred if it were held by laymen. Such property could only be conveyed to churches with prior express approval intended to protect against the loss of overlords' rights that would be compromised by the conveyance. Moreover, and more threatening, Philip IV launched an investigation into the then existing landed endowments of churches, obliging the institutions to produce proof that they had acquired their endowments legitimately, that is to say, that the lands were exempted, implicitly or explicitly, from providing whatever services might otherwise have been required. This was demanded, it was alleged, even if the churches had enjoyed long and peaceful possession of the properties. Lapses in the written record of proof were punishable by fine. Ecclesiastics were outraged, although a few ecclesiastics in Philip IV the Fair's inner circle actually helped to carry out the campaign.[67]

The French campaign was not unique; it closely resembles the more or less contemporary assault on mortmain in England, which was greeted with equal alarm by ecclesiastics.[68] Yet, it is a measure of how important it was to have been at the center of the effort to remake the kingdom of France by what I have called redemptive governance even three decades after the fact that in 1303, ten years into this prolonged and bitterly resented campaign, Philip IV stipulated that all the gifts that one Lord Simon de Nesle had given to churches were exempted from the restrictions and punitive fines for illicit endowments in mortmain. The king must have received a complaint from one of the recipients of Simon's largesse. How could he (Philip) trample on the deeds of a man (Simon) who had served the crown so well? The king relented, but he justified his exemption in more specific terms. His was a gift, he averred, to the memory of a man, Lord Simon de Nesle, who in his lifetime consecrated his services, merits, and devotion to Saint Louis, the now iconic incarnation of the dynasty's sacred character.[69]

Epilogue

My intention in the three short studies that have made up this book was to show that a biographical approach to the men around Louis IX might highlight certain central features of his rule and therefore of the temper of the realm in his reign. Louis IX instituted a genuinely repressive regime based on a narrow sense of what was morally permissible. Even behavior he objected to but did not criminalize, like singing profane songs, he stigmatized, tried to contain and ultimately to suppress. His behavior was not tempered by mercy when the issue was one of personal responsibility. The king could show love toward groups of marginal people, impoverished scholars, *béguines*, and those suffering ill treatment from his officials and servitors, to name three which I have discussed in this book. And a full treatment of his reign would show that this impulse extended to his treatment of penitent prostitutes and the creation of institutions to receive them and his treatment of the blind, lepers, and heretics' widows and orphans (as long as they were steadfastly orthodox in faith).[1] But toward transgressors—men and women who abused their social superiority or the administrative power the king vested in them—he was unforgiving. And he sought out men of similar outlook to punish those who could not restrain their transgressive impulses. He and these men whom he selected did not show compassion and mercy toward such individuals, but unrelentingly indulged the death penalty, public executions, and other humiliating forms of public justice to terrorize French society into moral behavior.

As Sophie Delmas has shown in her study of Eustache d'Arras, a professor and churchman whom Louis IX employed as an ambassador to the College of Cardinals, these ideas of kingship were constantly expressed in the court circle. Eustache preached several sermons before the king and his family in the course of his career.[2] To a certain extent the sentiments he expressed in these sermons were conventional. A king should imitate Christ, do justice, and preserve peace among Christians. A king should aspire to the highest form of the lay perfected life as the commander of the Christian host (*princeps exercitus christianorum*) against the enemies of the faith.[3] Yet Eustache did not confine his message to these generalities. In particular he stressed how a king was to do justice. It is a stark picture he paints, but one wholly in the service of Louis IX's own sensibility.

Those who would otherwise transgress should feel awe before royal righteousness. Fear was a necessary condition of justice. To this end, as Eustache mentions several times, a king should work closely with his *prévôt* (whom Delmas glosses as Étienne Boileau). If the king commands anyone's appearance on pain of death (*sub pena capitis*), he who was summoned should so fear the reality of the threat as to hasten to the ruler's presence before the wind has had a chance to change direction. Fear arises and ought to arise from knowledge of the king's and the *prévôt*'s enforcement of the law. So, "if anyone harbors thieves, what should the king do," Eustache asks. "He must surely hang him" is his reply: *Certe suspenderet ipsum.* And the *prévôt*, when he leads a thief to the gallows, should do so in a manner that publicly shames the blindfolded malefactor by dragging him through all the filth (*merdas*) in the city's streets. The blindfolding, it is perceived by the preacher, will increase the condemned man's fear and trepidation, since he will be unable to espy the gibbet and achieve even the minor comfort of knowing when his humiliation is nearing its end. The thief's accomplices, linked by rope and following behind their humiliated comrade, should be forced at the gallows to bind his hands for the hanging. And so it goes.[4] All of this, as Étienne Boileau would have been pleased to affirm, served the regime's aims of justice and peace.

To be sure, clergy could not carry out blood judgments. So men like Robert of Sorbon and Mathieu of Vendôme might agree with the king and laud his judicial severity without having to preside as a man or woman condemned to death suffered public hanging or burning or, as a lesser punishment, facial branding. Rather the clerics of the intimate inner circle, so many of whom were low-born, helped articulate the moral vision of a purified society and helped design the correctional institutions that addressed the alleged moral lesions of contemporary life. Even the king was apprehensive that not enough could be done or was being done or had been done to redeem the realm by the time he set out on his second crusade. Unrepentant prostitutes and blasphemers did not merely pollute the kingdom and elicit his and his regents' repression, they jeopardized the success of what was in Louis IX's moral universe the highest form of Catholic devotion, the willingness to die for Christ in the crusades. It is as if two choirs were in competition, indeed, were at war in the realm. One sang euphonious lauds to the Blessed Virgin Mary, the only true *Douce Dame*, the *Gloriosa domina*, and to the Holy and Undivided Trinity, the other was a cacophony of lyrics with sexually suggestive conceits and sacrilegious curses for refrains.

Those who shared the king's vision and whom he chose to be the vanguard in instituting it were in fact a motley group, whose social origins extended from peasants who had made good as churchmen to bourgeois to the highest aristocracy. Some were admitted to the most intimate circle of courtiers, but the courtiers themselves also needed to feel comfortable with all things aristocratic, and aristocrats in the court and aristocratic visitors to it had to feel that their self-worth was always recognized. Royal chaplains, even those by birth from families in the most abject poverty and natives of peripheral regions drawn to the court by means of networks of personal contacts, achieved a status which covered over low social origins, but it did not obliterate them. So, a man like Robert of Sorbon, at the center of one such network, could still suffer when a visitor like Jean de Joinville reminded him of where he came from and how far he was below an aristocrat like the *sénéchal* of Champagne. Those bourgeois who did not command the integument of clerical status were always a little sullied in the aristocracy's eyes and possibly even in Louis IX's by their concern for worldly riches. Perhaps this is why the king never seems to have admitted them to his inmost circle. When he wanted to bestow on them the benefits that came from intimacy, it was he himself who left the social space of the inner circle, as when he made a powerful statement of his support for Étienne Boileau by attending his court and sitting beside him while the *prévôt* handed down his pitiless sentences.

No one, I think, can know whether the men I have been discussing and the others who could be included in the group, like Mathieu of Vendôme and Philippe of Cahors, fully shared the king's vision. Did Simon de Nesle care anything for the *béguines* and the *Grand Béguinage*? It would have been easy enough to keep his mouth shut unless he was asked directly for his opinion, and if he had been asked, he could have uttered a lukewarm comment in favor of them or it without opposing the king or compromising his own position. But I do not think that Simon's passion lay with helping these women. If it had, he would have bequeathed them property in his will—and he did not, nor did his wife, even though they favored other institutions in Paris that the king was enthusiastic about. Any group of men of this sort had the potential of rubbing one another the wrong way. And we know there were plenty of criticisms of the king's own behavior. That which he knew about and he regarded as principled, he could and did learn from. But that which he thought was extreme, like Guillaume of Saint-Amour's, or that which offended his moral sensibilities, his idea of holy and decorous behavior, he rejected. The abrasions that must sometimes have manifested themselves among his courtiers and the wider circle of men he depended on, I do believe—and I hope I have shown or at least pointed to the possibility—he contained very well. The overall loyalty of these men to him and to his overarching ideal of rulership, indeed, was extraordinary.

Most common people—*le menu peuple*—knew of and admired perhaps one or more of the king's institutional gestures toward the poor and the marginalized. Or they knew of or had experienced the special courts of the *enquêteurs* where they could register complaints about bad administrative treatment. Or they knew of Louis IX's dedication to the struggle for Christian superiority in the East and supported him in it. True, occasionally they must have felt the sting of policies that they might otherwise praise. The crown's anti-Jewish measures, which I have written about at length were intended to protect *le menu peuple chrétien* from what was stigmatized as usury but may have been counterproductive in reducing the numbers of men and women who could provide needed consumption loans to poor people. Certainly this was a grievance writers claimed to have heard from people years later when Philip the Fair expelled the Jews.[5] And Parisian bourgeois—even some of the most pious among them, I will concede—must have been ambivalent about one of their own bearing the scars of the *fleur-de-lys* on his lips or having a neighbor woman's son of their class executed despite her pleas for mercy. It was good to have a thief off the streets, but did a mother's plaint count for nothing?

And it was no different at least in one respect for aristocrats who feared they were losing their power in their fiefs because of the treatment of Enguerrand de Coucy. Or perhaps they feared most that their bodies or their friends' bodies would be publicly humiliated if circumstances led them into trouble. One wonders sometimes—I wonder—what it must have been like for Queen Marguerite of Provence to plead unsuccessfully with her husband for the life of the lady of Pierrelaye or equally unsuccessfully for her execution behind closed doors. I wonder how Étienne Boileau explained his refusal to be merciful to his own godson's mother and to the friends and the kinfolk of his *compere* whom he also condemned to death. I wonder how Simon de Nesle dealt with the looks of the family of the young aristocrat who had without success implored him to rescind his order to execute their kinsman in public.

I even wonder how Robert of Sorbon felt as by most standards perfectly decent people in and around the royal household who happened to like a pretty song about profane love looked at him with resentment and shook their heads with disappointment at his contribution to the somberness of the court. I have in mind someone like the king's daughter Isabelle, who married

Count Thibaut V of Champagne, the same young man to whom the king had commended dressing well—dressing aristocratically—even though his own ascetic sensibility leaned toward plain garb. It was Thibaut with the future Philip III who had heard Jean de Joinville's sour exchange with Robert of Sorbon about appropriate dress, which in turn had led to the king's intervention to soften the *sénéchal*'s mockery of the secular master's peasant origins. Isabelle would have heard the story from her husband whom she married in 1255. She would have known a great deal about the rigorous moralist with whom her father kept company and their mutual contempt of vain songs. But she was the same girl, who appears to have relished such songs. Or at least a poet who wrote one in homage to her surpassing beauty (*k'il n'est si bele*), including her lips redder than a rose in May (*Les levres vermoilletes / Plus ke la rose n'est en mai*) must have imagined her appreciation of such songs. He wrote the song on the occasion of Isabelle's marriage to Thibaut at Melun and the nuptial celebrations at Provins thereafter.[6] What did such a woman think of a man like the great preacher who gave his name to the Sorbonne? And what did she want him to think of her?

There is so much still to wonder about these men at the center and their impress on those they sought to govern and to lead to salvation, so much, so very much.

109

Notes

Chapter One

[1] I have treated the matters discussed in this and the following paragraph while addressing the particular fate of one monastery in the region in Jordan, "Ardennais Monastery of Élan," 127–40.

[2] Many of the details on the life of Robert of Sorbon are drawn from volume I of Palémon Glorieux's *Aux origines de la Sorbonne*, which has the separate title *Robert de Sorbonne: l'homme, le collège, les documents*, 9–67. Félix Chambon's briefer sketch in his introductory remarks to his edition of Robert's *De Conscientia et De Tribus Dietis*, v–vii, is not always trustworthy on details, but remains useful, and I have used it with caution.

[3] Glorieux, *Aux origines de la Sorbonne*, I, 13–14; Ladvocat, *Dictionnaire historique-portatif*, II, 526.

[4] In referring to Robert as Robert of Sorbon I have adopted what I think is a valuable American convention. I use the English preposition 'of' before a place name that forms part of a northern French personal name when the person under discussion was non-noble, like Robert. I use the French form 'de' when the man or woman mentioned was of noble status. This is why the principal subject of Chapter Three is identified as Simon de Nesle. When referring to such nobles' lands apart from their personal names, however, I go back to 'of': Simon de Nesle is thus referred to interchangeably as the lord of Nesle. For the few nobles not of northern French birth mentioned in the book I adopt the traditional usage, 'of' (Blanche of Castile, Marguerite of Provence, and so forth).

[5] Glorieux, *Aux origines de la Sorbonne*, I, 14, 25–26, 30.

[6] Glorieux, *Aux origines de la Sorbonne*, I, 24–25; *Anciennes bibliothèques . . . Paris*, I, 222.

[7] Glorieux, *Aux origines de la Sorbonne*, I, 25.

[8] Glorieux, *Aux origines de la Sorbonne*, I, 48–51; Hauréau, "Propos de maître Robert de Sorbon," 141–48; Diekstra, "Robert de Sorbon's *Qui vult*," 215–72 (especially p. 257, "non deberet aliquis habere nomen Christiani et facere opera Sarraceni").

[9] Glorieux, *Aux origines de la Sorbonne*, I, 17–18.

[10] Among the materials for writing this are the succession of monuments erected in Sorbon—and their fate—as well as children's stories. For the former, see *Les Ardennes françaises*, no. 33 (September 1930), 551, and for an example of the latter, F.-C. Gérard's *Petit Jéhan*.

[11] Le Goff, *Saint Louis*, 425.

[12] On the whole experience of preaching as it pertains to Louis IX, see Jordan, "Louis IX: Preaching to Franciscan and Dominican Brothers and Nuns," 219–35; on the dialogical aspect, see p. 229.

[13] See Glorieux, *Aux origines de la Sorbonne*, I, 26–27, for an expert summary of Robert's views, abstracted from his treatises and sermons.

[14] Cf. *Anciennes bibliothèques . . . Paris*, I, 222. Glorieux, *Aux origines de la Sorbonne*, I, 29, is agnostic on the possible role of Count Robert d'Artois.

[15] Glorieux, *Aux origines de la Sorbonne*, I, 12 n. 6.

[16] Legros and Mathey-Maille, *Légende de Robert le Diable*; Herzman, Drake and Salisbury, "Havelock the Dane."

[17] Glorieux, *Aux origines de la Sorbonne*, I, 12 n. 6.

[18] Glorieux, *Aux origines de la Sorbonne*, I, 12 n. 6.

[19] Whether she was the author of the lyrics of the song, "Amours ou trop tard me sui pris," is still disputed, but the thirteenth-century attribution proves that her near contemporaries thought her capable of the composition. Sivéry, *Blanche de Castille*, 14 and 19; Maillard, *Roi-trouvère*, 27 and 67–68; Bédier, "Feuillet récemment retrouvé," 912–15.

[20] Glorieux, *Aux origines de la Sorbonne*, I, 28. See also *Anciennes bibliothèques . . . Paris*, I, 222.

[21] La Selle, "La confession et l'aumône," 262–63; La Selle, *Service des âmes à la cour*, 37, 40–42, 73, 99.

[22] Glorieux, *Aux origines de la Sorbonne*, I, 46. See also *Anciennes bibliothèques . . . Paris*, I, 222.

[23] *Anciennes bibliothèques . . . Paris*, I, 222.

[24] La Selle, *Service des âmes à la cour*, 41.

[25] Jordan, *Louis IX and the Challenge of the Crusade*, 65–104.

[26] Cf. Jean de Joinville, *Vie de saint Louis*, para. 140.

[27] Glorieux, *Aux origines de la Sorbonne*, I, 34-35. Cf. Chambon's remarks in Robert of Sorbon, *De conscientia et De Tribus Dietis*, vi.

[28] Glorieux, *Aux origines de la Sorbonne*, I, 33–38; *Anciennes bibliothèques . . . Paris*, I, 224.

[29] Jordan, *Louis IX*, 122.

[30] *Anciennes bibliothèques . . . Paris*, I, 225.

[31] Glorieux, *Aux origines de la Sorbonne*, I, 52–54; Delisle, *Cabinet des manuscrits*, II, 144–47, 149–50, 154, 157, 159, 161, 163–64, 170, 172–74, 178; *Anciennes bibliothèques . . . Paris*, I, 225; Chambon in Robert of Sorbon, *De Conscientia et De Tribus Dietis*, vi.

[32] Chambon in Robert of Sorbon, *De Conscientia et De Tribus Dietis*, vi.

[33] Jordan, *Louis IX*, 87–88.

[34] Lillich, *Gothic Stained Glass of Reims Cathedral*, 219.

[35] On the matters treated in this paragraph, see Jordan, *Tale of Two Monasteries*, 138–48.

[36] Moufflet, "Autour de l'Hôtel de saint Louis," 143–53.

[37] Jean talks about being acquainted with Louis for a good twenty-two years (*bien .xxii. ans en sa compaignie*), which would mean from the time he first met him until the king left on his last crusade; *Vie de saint Louis*, para. 686. Thus, *en sa compaignie* cannot mean at court (as a courtier), since for several years after their first meeting (paras. 93–97) they rarely if ever saw each other. Monfrin reproduces the Old French as modern French *en sa compagnie*. Smith's English translation in Joinville and Villehardouin, *Chronicles of the Crusades*, may mislead readers by rendering the phrase and similar phrases as "as a member of his entourage."

[38] Le Goff, *Saint Louis*, 680.

[39] For a succinct and persuasive assessment of the depth of Louis's commitment to the Cistercians and the mendicants, see Le Goff, *Saint Louis*, 746–50.

113

[40] For these anecdotes, see Jean de Joinville, *Vie de saint Louis*, paras. 31–32, 35–36, 38.

[41] But see Glorieux, *Aux origines de la Sorbonne*, I, 44–46, and Le Goff, *Saint Louis*, 485–86, 586 and 623.

[42] Bériou, "Robert de Sorbon," 469–510, including an edition of the texts.

[43] Hauréau, "Propos de maître Robert de Sorbon," 134, 137–41.

[44] Jean de Joinville, *Vie de saint Louis*, paras. 657–60. Note how Hugh strengthens *compaignie* by referring to people *en la court le roy en sa compaignie*, thereby making clear the difference between acquaintanceship, even fond acquaintanceship, and being continually in the royal entourage.

[45] Ladvocat, *Dictionnaire historique-portatif*, II, 527; *Anciennes bibliothèques . . . Paris*, I, 223–24. For Robert's wider contacts, who probably provided him moral support for his project and modest material support, see Glorieux, *Aux origines de la Sorbonne*, I, 34, 36, 42–43, 62.

[46] *Univers*, X: *Dictionnaire encyclopédique*, IX, 240.

[47] For most of this information in this paragraph, see *HL*, XIX, 359–60, 362 (the quotation on the quality of Guillaume's sermons is at 362). See also Glorieux, *Aux origines de la Sorbonne*, I, 33; Le Goff, *Saint Louis*, 193, 319, 335–36 and 748. On Guillaume's attempt to secure a position for his nephew at Saint-Denis, see *Série J, Trésor des chartes, supplément: Inventaire. J1028 à J1034*, J1030 no. 59.

[48] On Robert of Douai, see *Dictionnaire biographique des médicins*, II, 709–10. See also Glorieux, *Aux origines de la Sorbonne*, I, 33. Despite Wickersheimer's assertion, our Robert seems to be a different person from the contemporary Robert of Douai who was a clerk in the retinue of the prince of Achaia, one of the French principalities in crusader Greece; Glorieux, *Aux origines de la Sorbonne* , 47.

[49] See Paetow's annotations in Henri d'Andeli, *Battle of the Seven Arts*, 46 (citing the *Chartularium Universitatis Parisiensis*).

114

[50] Henri d'Andeli, *Battle of the Seven Arts*, 46–47; the identification of the character in the poem with Robert of Douai was made by the editor and translator Louis John Paetow.

[51] Wickersheimer, *Dictionnaire biographique des médicins*, 710.

[52] Duchesne, *Histoire de tous les cardinaux françois de naissance*, I, 304, and II, 228.

[53] Duchesne, *Histoire de tous les cardinaux françois de naissance*, I, 259–60; Ladvocat, *Dictionnaire historique-portatif*, II, 527.

[54] Jordan, "Case of Saint Louis," 215–16. Further on Louis IX's plain dress, as reflected in exactly contemporary royal art, see Lillich, *Gothic Stained Glass of Reims Cathedral*, 218.

[55] Jordan, *Louis IX*, 127-29, and Le Goff, *Saint Louis*, 757-60.

[56] Jordan, "Louis IX: Preaching to Franciscan and Dominican Brothers and Nuns," 226.

[57] For a spectrum of mostly agnostic views, see Maillard, *Roi-trouvère*, 27; O'Sullivan, "Putting Women in their Place," 92; Bec, "Accès au lieu érotique," 277.

[58] Huot, *Allegorical Play in the Old French Motet*, 108.

[59] Bartsch, "Geistliche Umdichtung," 573–76. There is a partial edition of ten of the sixteen verses in Maillard, "Roi-trouvère," 63–66.

[60] O'Sullivan, "Putting Women in their Place," 90–93; Maillard, *Roi-trouvère*, 66.

[61] For the dating, see O'Sullivan, "Putting Women in their Place," 84.

[62] O'Sullivan, "Putting Women in their Place," 92.

[63] I have followed O'Sullivan's transcription here ("Putting Women in their Place," 91). O'Sullivan reads *li* for Bartsch's *si* and *tegmine* for his *temigne* (see Bartsch, "Geistliche Umdichtung," 574, who does in fact query his own reading of *temigne*).

[64] The facsimile has been published as *Psautier de saint Louis*. The comprehensive study is Stahl's *Picturing Kingship*.

[65] "Now She is Martha, Now She is Mary: The Beguines of Medieval Paris."

[66] Stabler Miller, "What's in a Name? Clerical Representations of Parisian Beguines, 1200–1327," and idem, "Mirror of the Scholarly (Masculine) Soul: Thinking with Beguines in the Colleges of Medieval Paris."

[67] Stabler Miller, "What's in a Name?," 68; idem, "Mirror of the Scholarly (Masculine) Soul," 247–48.

[68] Stabler Miller, "What's in a Name?," 79–80.

[69] Stabler Miller, "What's in a Name?," 68.

[70] On the siting of the *béguinage* and the number of inmates, see Farmer, *Surviving Poverty in Medieval Paris*, p. 15 map and 143.

[71] Stabler Miller, "What's in a Name?," 68.

[72] Bériou, "Robert de Sorbon," 472.

[73] Stabler Miller, "What's in a Name?," 73–74 and 80; idem, "Mirror of the Scholarly (Masculine) Soul," 240–41, 245–46, 249–54.

[74] Bériou, "Robert de Sorbon," 477–79; Stabler Miller, "Mirror of the Scholarly (Masculine) Soul," 240.

[75] See Geltner's "Introduction" to William of Saint-Amour's *De periculis*, 1–18.

[76] Stabler Miller, "What's in a Name?," 69–82; idem, "Mirror of the Scholarly (Masculine) Soul," 249.

[77] Stabler Miller, "What's in a Name?," 75 and 79; idem, "Mirror of the Scholarly (Masculine) Soul," 247, 255–56; Bériou, "Robert de Sorbon," 471.

[78] Stabler Miller, "What's in a Name?," 62.

[79] Stabler Miller, "What's in a Name?," 84.

[80] Jean de Joinville, *Vie de saint Louis*, paras. 655–56.

[81] Jean de Joinville, *Vie de saint Louis*, paras. 30 and 718. See also Jordan, "Anti-Corruption Campaigns," 211.

[82] Leroux de Lincy, "Chansons historiques," 370–74 (I think the proper reading of the song is that its vitriol is directed at Louis IX's restrictive legislation rather than at the specific text, the *Établissements de saint Louis*, which Leroux de Lincy suggested).

[83] Leroux de Lincy, "Chansons historiques," 373–74.

[84] Leroux de Lincy, "Chansons historiques," 372.

[85] Leroux de Lincy, "Chansons historiques," 373–74.

[86] Leroux de Lincy, "Chansons historiques," 373.

[87] Leroux de Lincy, "Chansons historiques," 373.

Chapter Two

[1] Quoted with approval in Lespinasse and Bonnardot's edition of the *Livre des métiers*, xii.

[2] Chaix d'Est-Ange, *Dictionnaire des familles françaises anciennes et notables*, V, 36–39; Delisle, "Légendes sur la vie d'Étienne Boileau," 76.

[3] Louandre, *Mayeurs et maires d'Abbeville*, 65.

[4] Delisle, "Légendes sur la vie d'Étienne Boileau," 76–79; idem, "Chronologie des baillis et des sénéchaux," 25*–26*.

[5] Cf. Lespinasse and Bonnardot in *Livre des métiers*, xiv–xv n. 4.

[6] Lespinasse and Bonnardot in *Livre des métiers*, xiv–xv; Delisle, "Chronologie des baillis et des sénéchaux," 24*; Cazelles, *Nouvelle histoire de Paris*, 179.

[7] Gravier, "Essai sur les prévôts royaux," 539–74, 648–72, and 806–74.

[8] Jordan, *Louis IX*, 46–63 and 161–64; Sivéry, *Saint Louis et son siècle*, 282–85.

[9] Gravier, "Essai sur les prévôts royaux," 668.

[10] On central government and provincial (feudal) supreme courts, like the Exchequer of Normandy, see Jordan, *Louis IX*, 35–39 and 41 n. 28 (with references).

[11] Gravier, "Essai sur les prévôts royaux," 551–52; Jordan, *Louis IX*, 46–47, 161 and 168.

[12] Jordan, *Louis IX*, 162–63.

[13] Jordan, "Anti-Corruption Campaigns," 212–13; Jordan, *Louis IX*, 163–71.

[14] Jordan, *Louis IX*, 163–64.

[15] Lespinasse and Bonnardot in *Livre des métiers*, xv. See also Cazelles, *Nouvelle histoire de Paris*, 179.

[16] For the reference to him as a knight, see Delisle, "Chronologie des baillis et des sénéchaux," 25*. For a discussion of this characterization, see below.

[17] Delisle, "Chronologie des baillis et des sénéchaux," 23*.

[18] Sivêry, *Économie du royaume*, 14; Contamine and others, *Économie médiévale*, 214 and 272.

[19] Jean de Joinville, *Vie de saint Louis*, paras. 115–18.

[20] Jean de Joinville, *Vie de saint Louis*, paras. 115–18; the English is Smith's ("Life of Saint Louis").

[21] Jean de Joinville, *Vie de saint Louis*, paras. 715–18. I quote Smith's translation, "Life of Saint Louis," with a few modifications in brackets.

[22] "Extraits des Chroniques de Saint-Denis," 117–18.

[23] Borelli de Serres, *Recherches sur divers services publics du XIIIe au XVIIe siècle*.

[24] On my behalf, my graduate student Jenna Phillips carried out the research into this archive and its access in November 2011.

[25] Borelli de Serres, *Recherches sur divers services publics du XIIIe au XVIIe siècle*, I, 531–72.

[26] Jordan, *Louis IX*, 171–81.

[27] Serper, "Administration royale de Paris," 123–39.

[28] Serper, "Administration royale de Paris," 129–32.

[29] Gauvard, *Crime, état et société*, I, 232–33.

[30] Cazelles, *Nouvelle histoire de* Paris, 178.

[31] Bove, *Dominer la ville*, 188–99. For a slight dissent, which in no way affects his overall purchase of Borrelli de Serres' views, see p. 190.

[32] Bove, *Dominer la ville*, 195.

[33] Bove, *Dominer la ville*, 195.

[34] On Mathieu's career, see Jordan, *A Tale of Two Monasteries*, passim.

[35] Le Goff, *Saint Louis*, 237–38, 664; Delisle, "Chronologie des baillis et des sénéchaux," 23*. The *Livre des métiers* was edited and published by Lespinasse and Bonnardot.

[36] Jordan, *Louis IX*, 173 n. 234.

[37] Delisle, "Chronologie des baillis et des sénéchaux," 23*–24* on the central role of Étienne Boileau in the reform; his criticisms of Borelli de Serres are too numerous to list.

[38] Le Goff, *Saint Louis*, 237 n. 1; Richard, *Saint Louis*, 298.

[39] Bove, *Dominer la ville*, 196.

[40] Jordan, *Louis IX*, 47.

[41] Jordan, *Louis IX*, 51–53, 153–54.

[42] Jordan, "Anti-Corruption Campaigns," 211.

[43] "Extraits d'une chronique anonyme," 141.

[44] Tanon, *Histoire des justices*, 1–15.

[45] Delisle, "Chronologie des baillis et des sénéchaux," 21*–22*; Bove, *Dominer la ville*, 665.

[46] Cf. Cazelles, *Nouvelle histoire de Paris*, 177–78; Cazelles does not retell the story but notes the inefficiencies of government in Paris before the crusade.

[47] "Extraits d'une chronique anonyme," 141.

[48] Duby, *Chivalrous Society*, 112–22.

[49] "Extraits d'une chronique anonyme," 141.

[50] Le Goff, *Saint Louis*, 689. Bove, *Dominer la ville*, 186, speculates that there may have been bourgeois courtiers, left unrecorded in sources, which are biased toward clerics and aristocrats.

[51] Jordan, *Louis IX*, 177.

[52] Quoted in the introduction to the *Livre des métiers*, xii.

[53] *Recueil des chartes . . . Saint-Martin-des-Champs*, V, 59–60 no. 1188 (dated 1264).

[54] "Extraits d'une chronique anonyme," 141.

[55] "Extraits des Chroniques de Saint-Denis," 118.

[56] "Extraits des Chroniques de Saint-Denis," 118.

[57] Jordan, *Louis IX*, 175–81; Richard, *Saint Louis*, 299. See also Serper, 132–39; Le Goff, *Saint Louis*, 237 and 663–64; Bove, *Dominer la ville*, 193–94.

[58] This house is mentioned several times in the criminal records from 1263 through 1266; *Registre criminel de Sainte-Geneviève*, 356–58.

[59] *Registre criminel de Sainte-Geneviève*, 357–58.

[60] Ogerius Alferius, "Chronicon astense," cols. 142–43. See also Guillelmus Ventura, "Memoriale de gestis civium Astensium," col. 189.

[61] Grunwald, "Lombards, Cahorsins and Jews," 396–97; Nada Patrone and Airaldi, *Comuni e signorie nell'Italia settentrionale*, 180.

[62] The identification of Guido Livardi as an Astigian or from the commune's hinterland depends on his name, Livardi being a variant of Bardi. Bardi was a commune on the Emilia-Romagna march with Piedmont.

[63] Cf. Le Goff, *Saint Louis*, 235–36. The most comprehensive treatment of the economy is Sivéry, *Économie du royaume de France au siècle de saint Louis*.

[64] Delisle, "Chronologie des baillis et sénéchaux," 25*.

[65] Jordan, *Louis IX*, 118.

[66] Delisle, "Chronologie des baillis et des sénéchaux," 26*. For some information on the later career of Philippe of Cahors, see Carolus-Barré, *Procès de canonisation*, 146, 211, 214, 263 n. 17.

[67] Delisle, "Chronologie des baillis et des sénéchaux," 25*.

[68] Delisle, "Chronologie des baillis et de sénéchaux," 25*.

[69] Giry, *Manuel de diplomatique*, I, 331.

[70] Rogozinski, "Ennoblement by the Crown," 273–91.

[71] Cazelles, *Nouvelle histoire de Paris*, 179.

[72] Bove, *Dominer la ville*, 194; Delisle, "Chronologie des baillis et des sénéchaux," 25*.

[73] Sivéry, *Saint Louis et son siècle*, 582; idem, *Philippe III*, 206.

Chapter Three

[1] Carolus-Barré, *Procès de canonisation*, 168; Newman, *Seigneurs de Nesle*, I, 50.

[2] Carolus-Barré, *Procès de canonisation*, 170; Newman, *Seigneurs de Nesle*, I, 51, regularly assigned her the name Adèle, although the texts he edited in volume II speak of her as Alix. In the headnotes

to one charter (II, 310 no. 201) Newman was inconsistent and used Alice.

[3] Strayer, *Albigensian Crusades*, 54-136.

[4] Sivéry, *Blanche de Castille*, 179.

[5] Carolus-Barré, *Procès de canonisation*, 169; Sivéry, *Philippe III*, 94.

[6] There is abundant material to help understand the situation in the Franco-Flemish borderlands in this period in Baldwin, *Government of Philip Augustus*, 3–27 and 19–219. Spiegel, *Romancing the Past*, addresses the ideological choices and their impact on the texts created in aristocratic circles in the borderlands.

[7] Sivéry invokes this fact virtually as a mantra, although it may not bear all the explanatory power he implies by the repetition; *Philippe III*, 41, 94, 219, etc.

[8] On the mythography of the battle, see Duby, *Legend of Bouvines*, and Jordan, "French Victory at Bouvines," 113–28. On the specific role of Jean de Nesle in the battle and its aftermath, see Baldwin, *Government of Philip Augustus*, 219; Spiegel, *Romancing the Past*, 48.

[9] Sivéry, *Blanche de Castille*, 103; Carolus-Barré, *Procès de canonisation*, 169.

[10] Carolus-Barré, *Procès de canonisation*, 170; Sivéry, *Marguerite de Provence*, 33–35.

[11] Giry, *Manuel de diplomatique*, 328 n. 2.

[12] Carolus-Barré, *Procès de canonisation*, 170.

[13] Carolus-Barré, *Procès de canonisation*, 170, notes Simon's role as an adviser.

[14] Jordan, *Louis IX*, 113–16; Barber, "Crusade of the Shepherds," 1–23.

[15] Jordan, *Louis IX*, 117–19.

[16] Carolus-Barré, *Procès de canonisation*, 171; Newman, *Seigneurs de Nesle*, I, 51.

[17] Richard, *Saint Louis*, 260–61; Jordan, *Louis IX*, 124–25.

[18] Carolus-Barré, *Procès de canonisation*, 171.

[19] Carolus-Barré, *Procès de canonisation*, 171; Carolus-Barré, "Saint Louis et les translations des corps saints," 1087–1112.

121

[20] Sivéry, *Saint Louis et son siècle*, 602–03; Richard, *Saint Louis*, 356–59; Carolus-Barré, *Procès de canonisation*, 171; Newman, *Seigneurs de Nesle*, I, 51; Jordan, *Louis IX*, 199–200.

[21] Jordan, *Tale of Two Monasteries*, 1–3.

[22] Carolus-Barré, *Procès de canonisation*, 171; Newman, *Seigneurs de Nesle*, I, 51; Jordan, *Tale of Two Monasteries*, 49–65.

[23] Richard, *Saint Louis*, 367.

[24] Carolus-Barré, *Procès de canonisation*, 81–82.

[25] Richard, *Saint Louis*, 305–6.

[26] Le Goff, *Saint Louis*, 861–62.

[27] Carolus-Barré, *Procès de canonisation*, 82.

[28] Le Goff, *Saint Louis*, 862; Carolus-Barré, *Procès de canonisation*, 82–83.

[29] Jordan, *Louis IX*, 208–9, with references to other bibliography. See also idem, *Tale of Two Monasteries*, 77 and 203, and Leson, "Heraldry and Identity," 162 and notes at 191.

[30] Richard, *Saint Louis*, 374–75; Carolus-Barré, *Procès de canonisation*, 79–81.

[31] Carolus-Barré, *Procès de canonisation*, 172; Newman, *Seigneurs de Nesle*, I, 52.

[32] Carolus-Barré, *Procès de canonisation*, 172; Newman, *Seigneurs de Nesle*, I, 52.

[33] Carolus-Barré, *Procès de canonisation*, 172.

[34] Newman, *Seigneurs de Nesle*, I, 51–52. For the varied functions of *Parlement* under Louis IX, see Bisson, "Consultative Functions," 357–63.

[35] Jordan, *Tale of Two Monasteries*, 67–72 and 130.

[36] Newman, *Seigneurs de Nesle*, I, 52–53.

[37] Carolus-Barré, *Procès de canonisation*, 173.

[38] Jordan, *Tale of Two Monasteries*, 131–35.

[39] Jordan, *Tale of Two Monasteries*, 25.

[40] Jordan, *Tale of Two Monasteries*, 25.

[41] This was the sentiment he expressed after his defeat in 1250; Jordan, *Louis IX*, 127.

[42] Jordan, *Tale of Two Monasteries*, 132. Cf. Le Goff, *Saint Louis*, 291–92; Richard, *Saint Louis*, 557.

[43] Jean de Joinville, *Vie de saint Louis*, para. 686. I quote the same paragraph from Smith's translation, "Life of Saint Louis."

[44] Jean de Joinville, *Vie de saint Louis*, para. 685. Again, I quote Smith's translation, "Life of Saint Louis."

[45] Fawtier, "Un compte de menues dépenses," 24 and 26 nos. 174 and 194.

[46] Jordan, "Fresh Look at Medieval Sanctuary," 25.

[47] O'Sullivan, "Putting Women in their Place," 92.

[48] Cf. his attitude to the French royal *fleur-de-lysée* coronation robe; Lillich, *Gothic Stained Glass of Reims Cathedral*, 218.

[49] Jordan, *Tale of Two Monasteries*, 131–35.

[50] Newman, *Seigneurs de Nesle*, I, 53–54.

[51] Jordan, *Tale of Two Monasteries*, 141.

[52] Newman, *Seigneurs de Nesle*, I, 54.

[53] Carolus-Barré, *Procès de canonisation*, 173; Newman, *Seigneurs de Nesle*, I, 54; Jordan, *Tale of Two Monasteries*, 211–12.

[54] Jordan, *Tale of Two Monasteries*, 135–36; Carolus-Barré, *Procès de canonisation*, 172; Newman, *Seigneurs de Nesle*, I, 56.

[55] Carolus-Barré, *Procès de canonisation*, 79–89, 223–36; Jordan, *Tale of Two Monasteries*, 202–03.

[56] Carolus-Barré, *Procès de canonisation*, 173; Newman, *Seigneurs de Nesle*, I, 54.

[57] Carolus-Barré, *Procès de canonisation*, 173; *Chartrier de l'Abbaye-aux[-]Bois*, p. 344.

[58] Carolus-Barré, *Procès de canonisation*, 173; Newman, *Seigneurs de Nesle*, I, 54–55; Jordan, *Tale of Two Monasteries*, 214.

[59] Jordan, *Tale of Two Monasteries*, 212–14.

[60] Jordan, *Tale of Two Monasteries*, 214.

[61] Carolus-Barré, *Procès de canonisation*, 174; Jordan, *Tale of Two Monasteries*, 214.

[62] *Chartrier de l'Abbaye-aux[-]Bois*, 344–47; Newman, *Seigneurs de Nesle*, II, 352–55 no. 218.

[63] Newman, *Seigneurs de Nesle*, I, 57.

[64] Jordan, *Louis IX*, 185 and 190.

[65] Newman, *Seigneurs de Nesle*, II, 329–42 no. 212.

[66] *Chartrier de l'Abbaye-aux[-]Bois*, 346, "Encore ordenne je et eslis executeur principal deseur touz de chest mien testament honme religieus et honeste mon chier ami Mathieu, par le grace de Dieu abbé de Saint Denis en France."

[67] Jordan, *Unceasing Strife*, 59–60 and 82–83.

[68] Jordan, *Tale of Two Monasteries*, 178.

[69] Carolus-Barré, *Procès de canonisation*, 175.

Epilogue

[1] The most comprehensive treatment to date is Le Goff's *Saint Louis*.

[2] Delmas, *Un Franciscain à Paris*, pp. 17, 263–66, 171–72, 294–301.

[3] Delmas, *Un Franciscain à Paris*, pp. 266–67.

[4] For the quotations, see Delmas, *Un Franciscain à Paris*, p. 267 nn. 2–7.

[5] On Louis IX's anti-Jewish policies, see my *French Monarchy and the Jews*, 128–50; for criticisms of Philip IV's expulsion on the grounds of its financial impact on poor people, see, p. 215.

[6] Meyer, "Chanson française en l'honneur d'Isabelle, fille de saint Louis," 1–5.

124

List of References

Primary Sources

Actes du Parlement de Paris. 2 vols. Ed. Edgar Boutaric. Paris: Henri Plon, 1863–1867.

Bartsch, K. "Geistliche Umdichtung weltlicher Lieder." *Zeitschrift für romanische Philologie* 8 (1884): 570–85.

Bédier, Joseph. "Un feuillet récemment retrouvé d'un chansonnier français du XIIIe siècle." In *Mélanges de philologie romane et d'histoire littéraire offerts à M. Maurice Wilmotte*, 2 vols., 895–922. Paris: Honoré Champion, 1910.

Bériou, Nicole. "Robert de Sorbon, le prud'homme et le béguin, suivi d'Appendice I et II." *Comptes-rendus des séances de l'Académie des Inscriptions et Belles-Lettres* 138 (1994): 469–510.

Chartrier de l'Abbaye-aux[-]Bois (1202–1341): Étude et édition. Edited by Brigitte Pipon. Paris: École des chartes, 1996.

d'Andeli, Henri. *The Battle of the Seven Arts.* Edited and translated by Louis Paetow. Berkeley: University of California Press, 1914.

"Extraits des Chroniques de Saint-Denis." In *Recueil des historiens des Gaules et de la France*, XXI, 103–23. Paris: Imprimerie Impériale, 1855.

"Extraits d'un chronique anonyme, finissant en M.CCC.LXXX." In *Recueil des historiens des Gaules et de la France*, XXI, 141. Paris: Imprimerie Impériale, 1855.

Guillelmus Ventura. "Memoriale de gestis civium Astensium et plurimum illorum." In *Annali d'Italia dal principio dell'era volgare sino all' anno MDCCXLIX*, edited by Lodovico Muratori. 18 vols. XI, cols. 153–268. Milan: Società Tipografica de' Classici Italiani, 1818–1821.

Joinville, Jean de. *Vie de saint Louis.* Edited and translated by Jacques Monfrin. Paris: Garnier, 1995.

—. "The Life of Saint Louis." Translated by Caroline Smith. In Joinville and Villehardouin. *Chronicles of the Crusades*, 137–336. Penguin: London, 2008.

125

Leroux de Lincy [Antoine]. "Chansons historiques des XIIIe, XIVe et XVe siècles." *Bibliothèque de l'École des chartes* 1 (1839–1840): 359–88.

Maillard, Jean. *Roi-trouvère du XIIIème siècle: Charles d'Anjou.* [Dallas]: American Institute of Musicology, 1967.

Métiers et corporations de la ville, XIIIe siècle: Le Livre des métiers d'Étienne Boileau. Edited by René de Lespinasse and François Bonnardot. Paris: Imprimerie nationale, 1879.

Meyer, Paul. "Chanson française en l'honneur d'Isabelle, fille de saint Louis." *Annuaire-bulletin de la Société de l'histoire de France* 2 (1864), section 2: 1–5.

Newman, William. *Les seigneurs de Nesle* (see below, under secondary sources).

Ogerius Alferius. "Chronicon Astense." In *Annali d'Italia dal principio dell'era volgare sino all' anno MDCCXLIX.* Edited by Lodovico Muratori, 18 vols. XI, cols. 139–52. Milan: Società Tipografica de' Classici Italiani, 1818–1821.

Olim (Les) ou registres des arrêts rendus par la cour du roi. I: *1254–1273.* Edited by Auguste-Arthur Beugnot. Paris: Imprimerie royale, 1839.

Psautier de saint Louis, Le. Edited by Marcel Thomas. Graz: Akademische Druck- und Verlagsanstalt, 1970.

Recueil de chartes et documents de Saint-Martin-des-Champs: monastère parisien, V. Edited by J. Depoin. Paris: A. Picard et fils, 1921.

Registre criminel de Sainte-Geneviève. In Louis Tanon, *Histoire des justices des anciennes églises et communautés de Paris,* 347–412. Paris: L. Larose and Forcel, 1883.

Robert of Sorbon. *De Conscientia et De Tribus Dietis.* Edited by Félix Chambon. Paris: Alphonse Picard et Fils, 1902.

Série J, Trésor des chartes, supplément: Inventaire. J1028 à J1034. Comp. Henri de Curzon. On-line at http://www. archivesnationales.culture.gouv.fr/chan/chan/fonds/EGF/SA/ InvSAPDF/SA_index_J/J_suppl_pdf/J1028_1034.pdf

William of Saint-Amour. *De periculis novissimorum temporum.* Edited and translated by G[uy] Geltner. Paris and elsewhere: Peeters, 2008.

Secondary Sources

Anciennes bibliothèques des églises, monastères, collèges, etc., I: *Les anciennes bibliothèques de Paris*, I. Alfred Franklin. Paris: Imprimerie Impériale, 1867.

Baldwin, John. *The Government of Philip Augustus: Foundations of French Royal Power in the Middle Ages.* Berkeley and Los Angeles: University of California Press, 1986.

Barber, Malcolm. "The Crusade of the Shepherds." In *Proceedings of the Tenth Annual Meeting of the Western Society for French History*, 1–23. Lawrence, KS: University Press of Kansas, 1984.

Bec, Pierre. "L'accès au lieu érotique: motifs et exorde dans la lyrique popularisante du moyen âge à nos jours." In *Love and Marriage in the Twelfth Century*, edited by Willy van Hoecke et al., 250–99. Louvain/Leuven: Presses Universitaires de Louvain/Leuven University Press, 1981.

Bisson, Thomas. "Consultative Functions in the King's Parlements (1250–1314)." *Speculum* 44 (1969): 353–73.

Borelli de Serres, Léon-Louis. *Recherches sur divers services publics du XIIIe au XVIIe siècle.* 3 vols. Paris: A. Picard et fils, 1895–1909.

Bove, Boris. *Dominer la ville: prévôts des marchands et échevins parisiens de 1260 à 1350.* Paris: Comité des travaux historiques et scientifiques, 2004.

Carolus-Barré, Louis. *Le procès de canonisation de saint Louis (1272-1297): essai de reconstitution.* Rome: École française de Rome, 1994.

—. "Saint Louis et la translation des corps saints." In *Études d'histoire du droit canonique (dédiées à Gabriel Le Bras)*, II, 1087–1112. Paris: Sirey, 1965.

Cazelles, Raymond. *Nouvelle histoire de Paris de la fin du règne de Philippe Auguste à la mort de Charles VI, 1223–1380*. Paris: Hachette, 1994.

Chaix d'Est-Ange, Gustave. *Dictionnaire des familles françaises anciennes et notables à la fin du XIXe siècle*. 20 vols. Évroux: C. Hérissey, 1903–1929.

Contamine, Philippe, et al. *L'économie médiévale*. Paris: A. Colin, 1993.

Delisle, Léopold. *Le Cabinet des manuscrits de la Bibliothèque nationale*, II. Paris: Imprimerie Nationale, 1874.

—. "Chronologie des baillis et des sénéchaux." In *Recueil des histories des Gaules et de la France*, XXIV. 15*-270*. Paris: Imprimerie nationale, 1904.

—. "Légendes sur la vie d'Étienne Boileau," *Bulletin de la Société de l'histoire de Paris et de l'Ile-de-France* 29 (1902): 76–79.

Delmas, Sophie. *Un Franciscain à Paris au milieu du XIII siècle: le maître en théologie Eustache d'Arras*. Paris: Éditions du Cerf, 2010.

Diekstra, F. N. M. "Robert de Sorbon *Qui vult vere confiteri* (ca. 1260–1274) and Its French Versions." *Recherches de théologie ancienne et médiévale* 60 (1993): 215–72.

Duby, Georges. *The Chivalrous Society*. Translated by Cynthia Postan. Berkeley and Los Angeles: University of California Press, 1977.

—. *The Legend of Bouvines: War, Religion and Culture in the Middle Ages*. Translated by Catherine Tihanyi. Cambridge: Polity Press, 1990.

Duchesne, François. *Histoire de tous les cardinaux françois de naissance*. 2 vols. Paris: Privately printed, 1660.

Durbin, Bertrand. *La crise du logement des étudiants à Paris au XIIIème siècle*. Thèse-mémoire Université Panthéon-ASSAS (Paris II), Droit-Économie-Sciences Sociales, année universitaire 2005–2005, on-line http://www.princeton.edu/main/news/bulletin/docs/Bulletin-2011-06-13.pdf

128

Farmer, Sharon. *Surviving Poverty in Medieval Paris: Gender, Ideology, and the Daily Lives of the Poor*. Ithaca, NY, and London: Cornell University Press, 2002.

Fawtier, Robert. "Un compte de menues dépenses de l'Hôtel du roi Philippe VI le Valois pour le premier semestre de l'année 1337." In *Autour de la France capétienne: personnages et institutions*, edited by Jeanne Stone. London: Variorum Reprints, 1987. Essay XVI.

Gauvard, Claude. *De grace especial: crime, état et société en France à la fin du Moyen âge*. 2 vols. Paris: Publications de la Sorbonne, 1991.

Gérard, F.-C. *Le Petit Jéhan: histoire d'un écolier de Paris*. Rouen: Mégard, 1856.

Giry, A[rthur]. *Manuel de diplomatique*. 2 vols. New ed. Paris: F. Alcan, 1925.

Glorieux, Palémon. *Aux origines de la Sorbonne*. 2 vols. Paris: J. Vrin, 1965–1966.

—. *Les origines du Collège de Sorbonne*. (Texts and Studies in the History of Mediaeval Education 8). Notre Dame, IN: Mediaeval Institute, University of Notre Dame, 1959.

Gravier, Henri. "Essai sur les prévôts royaux du XIe au XIVe siècle." *Nouvelle revue historique de droit français et étranger* 27 (1903): 539–74, 648–72, 806–74.

Grunwald, Kurt. "Lombards, Cahorsins and Jews." *Journal of European Economic History* 4 (1975): 393–98.

Hauréau, [Jean-]B[arthélemy]. "Les propos de maître Robert de Sorbon." *Mémoires de l'Institut de France* 31 (1884): 133–49.

Herzman, Ronald, Graham Drake and Eve Salisbury, eds. "Havelok the Dane." Originally published in *Four Romances of England*. Kalamazoo, MI: Medieval Institute Publications, 1999. On-line http://www.lib.rochester.edu/camelot/teams/danefrm.htm

Histoire littéraire de la France. 42 vols. to date. New ed. Paris: V. Palmé, 1865-.

129

Huot, Sylvia. *Allegorical Play in the Old French Motet: The Sacred and the Profane in Thirteenth-Century Polyphony.* Stanford: Stanford University Press, 1997.

Jordan, William. "Anti-Corruption Campaigns in Thirteenth-Century Europe." *Journal of Medieval History* 35 (2009): 204–19.

—. "The Ardennais Monastery of Élan in the Late Twelfth and Early Thirteenth Century," *Cîteaux: Commentarii cistercienses* 61 (2010): 127–40.

—. "The Case of Saint Louis," *Viator* 19 (1988): 209–17.

—. "The French Victory at Bouvines (1214) and the Persistent Seduction of War." In *1212–1214: el trienio que hizo a Europa.* Pamplona: Gobierno de Navarra, 2011.

—. "A Fresh Look at Medieval Sanctuary." In *Law and the Illicit in Medieval Europe*, edited by Ruth Karras, Joel Kaye, and E. Ann Matter, 17–32. Philadelphia: University of Pennsylvania Press, 2008.

—. *Louis IX and the Challenge of the Crusade: A Study in Rulership.* Princeton: Princeton University Press, 1979.

—. "Louis IX: Preaching to Franciscan and Dominican Brothers and Nuns." In *Defenders and Critics of Franciscan Life: Essays in Honor of John V. Fleming*, edited by Michael Cusato and Guy Geltner, 219–35. Brill: Leiden and Boston, 2009.

—. *A Tale of Two Monasteries: Westminster and Saint-Denis in the Thirteenth Century.* Princeton: Princeton University Press, 2009.

—. *Unceasing Strife, Unending Fear: Jacques de Thérines and the Freedom of the Church in the Age of the Last Capetians.* Princeton: Princeton University Press, 2005.

Ladvocat, Jean-Baptiste. *Dictionnaire historique-portatif*, II. New ed. Paris: Didot, 1755.

La Selle, Xavier de. "La confession et l'aumône: confesseurs et aumôniers des rois de France du XIIIe au XVe siècle." *Journal des savants*, July–December (1993): 255–86.

—. *Le service des âmes à la cour: confesseurs et aumôniers des rois de France du XIIIe au XVe siècle.* Paris: École des chartes, 1995.

130

Le Goff, Jacques. *Saint Louis*. Paris: Gallimard, 1996.

Legros, Huguette, and Laurence Mathey-Maille, eds. *La légende de Robert le Diable du moyen âge au XXe siècle: actes du colloque international de l'Université de Caen des 17 et 18 septembre 2009.* Orléans: Editions Paradigme, 2010.

Leson, Richard. "Heraldry and Identity in the Psalter-Hours of Jeanne of Flanders (Manchester, John Rylands Library, MS Lat. 117)." *Studies in Iconography* 32 (2011): 155–98.

Lillich, Meredith. *The Gothic Stained Glass of Reims Cathedral.* University Park, PA: Pennsylvania State University Press, 2011.

Louandre, François-César. *Les mayeurs et maires d'Abbeville: 1184–1847.* Abbeville: T. Jeunet, 1851.

Moufflet, Jean-François. "Autour de l'Hôtel de saint Louis (1226–1270): le cadre, les hommes, les itineraries d'un pouvoir." In *Positions des thèses soutenues par les élèves de la promotion de 2007 pour obtenir le diplôme d'archiviste paléographe*, 143–53. Paris: École nationale des chartes, 2007.

Nada Patrone, Anna Maria, and Gabriella Airaldi. *Comuni et signorie nell'Italia settentrionale: il Piemonte et la Liguria.* Turin: UTET, 1986.

Newman, William. *Les Seigneurs de Nesle en Picardie (XIIe–XIIIe siècle): leurs chartes et leur histoire.* 2 vols. Paris: A. et J. Picard, 1971.

O'Sullivan, Daniel. "Putting Women in their Place: Women's Devotional Songs in the *Rosarius* (BnF fr. 12483)." In *Dialogism and Lyric Self-Fashioning: Bakhtin and the Voices of a Genre*, edited by Jacob Blevins, 84–94. Selinsgrove, PA: Susquehanna University Press, 2008.

Richard, Jean. *Saint Louis: roi d'une France féodale, soutien de la Terre sainte.* Paris: Fayard, 1983.

Rogozinski, Jan. "Ennoblement by the Crown and Social Stratification in France, 1285–1322." In *Order and Innovation in the Middle Ages: Essays in Honor of Joseph R. Strayer*, edited by William Jordan, C. Bruce McNab, and Teofilo Ruiz, 273–91. Princeton: Princeton University Press, 1976.

Serper, Arié. "L'administration royale de Paris au temps de Louis IX." *Francia* 7 (1979): 123–39.

Sivéry, Gérard. *Blanche de Castille*. Paris: Fayard, 1990.

—. *L'économie du royaume de France au siècle de saint Louis (vers 1180-vers 1315)*. Lille: Presses Universitaires de Lille, 1984.

—. *Marguerite de Provence: une reine au temps des cathédrales*. Paris: Fayard, 1987.

—. *Philippe III le Hardi*. Paris: Fayard, 2003.

—. *Saint Louis et son siècle*. Paris: Tallandier, 1983.

Spiegel, Gabrielle. *Romancing the Past: The Rise of Vernacular Prose Historiography in Thirteenth-Century France*. Berkeley, Los Angeles and Oxford: University of California Press, 1993.

Stabler Miller, Tanya. "Mirror of the Scholarly (Masculine) Soul: Thinking with Beguines in the Colleges of Medieval Paris." In *Negotiating Clerical Identities: Priests, Monks, and Masculinity in the Middle Ages*, edited by Jennifer Thibodeaux, 238–64. New York: Palgrave Macmillan, 2010.

—. "Now She is Martha, Now She is Mary: The Beguines of Medieval Paris." Ph. D. Dissertation in History, University of California at Santa Barbara, 2007.

—. "What's in a Name? Clerical Representations of Parisian Beguines, 1200–1327." *Journal of Medieval History* 33 (2007): 60–86.

Stahl, Harvey. *Picturing Kingship: History and Painting in the Psalter of Saint Louis*. University Park, PA: The Pennsylvania State University Press, 2008.

Strayer, Joseph. *The Albigensian Crusades*. New York: Dial Press, 1971.

Tanon, Louis. *Histoire des justices des anciens églises et communautés monastiques de Paris*. Paris: L. Larose and Forcel, 1883.

Univers, L': Histoire et description de tous les peoples, X—Dictionnaire encyclopédique de la France, IX. Comp. Phillipe Le Bas. Paris: F. Didot Frères, 1843.

Wickersheimer, Ernest. Dictionnaire biographique des médicins en France au moyen âge. 2 vols. Geneva: Librarie Droz, 1979.

Index

133

135